13-MOON DIARY
OF NATURAL TIME

Child of the Earth,

Grandchild of the Sun,

Great-grandchild of Grandmother Galaxy

Know the Spirit of Time

If you do not know about time,

You cannot know who you are.

To know who you are

Is to know how to take your time.

Be who you are, time is yours to know

Hold steady as you go, it's all in the flow

- from: Turtle and Tree by José Argüelles -

Cover:

The Moon Goddess is sitting on the sickle holding a rabbit in her arms. She is surrounded by the 13-Moon animals of the 13-Moon Calendar in the sickle of a blue moon against a starry sky. The Moon is the opposite of the Earth. She keeps us in balance. She takes care of our soil hydrology, whereas not a drop of water can be found on her. When there are forest fires and our planet seems to be orange, the Moon seems to be blue. That is when this photograph was taken. The Moon Goddess of the ancient Maya - Ixchel or Ixquic - resided on the Moon, sitting on the sickle. She held a rabbit in her arms. Young Ixquic and her son Ixbalanqué often appeared to people as rabbits or hares. The Maya also recognized the profile of a rabbit in the dark spots on the Moon.

A Way to Live the Ancient Maya Calendar

13-MOON DIARY
OF NATURAL TIME

December 30, 2005 - July 25, 2007
or
Moon 7 of Yellow Cosmic Seed Year
until Red Magnetic Moon Year

Frontier Publishing

Title: 13-MOON DIARY OF NATURAL TIME - A Way to Live the Ancient Maya Calendar
2006 - July 2007

© 2005 Nicole E. Zonderhuis and Sylvia Carrilho

Concept & design: Sylvia Carrilho and Nicole E. Zonderhuis
Text: Nicole E. Zonderhuis
Cover design & illustrations: Nicole E. Zonderhuis
Initiative: Sylvia Carrilho
Layout: Buro Kunst en Drukwerk, Sylvia Carrilho
Translation: Janet Ossebaard

ISBN 90 8067 009 X

Frontier Publishing
P.O. Box 10681
1001 ER AMSTERDAM
the Netherlands
Tel. +31-(0)20-3309151
Fax +31-(0)20-3309150
E-mail: info@fsf.nl
www.frontierpublishing.nl

Adventures Unlimited Press
303 Main St., P.O. Box 74
Kempton, IL 60946, USA
Tel: 815-253-6390
Fax: 815-253-6300
E-mail: auphq@frontiernet.net
www.adventuresunlimitedpress.com

Contents

This diary is a combination of the Gregorian Calendar and the 13-Moon Calendar or Dreamspell Calendar by José Argüelles. With this desk diary you can see at a glance what day it is, both according to the Gregorian Calendar and the 13-Moon Calendar. The seal of the day is represented as a pictograph, right next to the 'ordinary' date. You can find the meaning of the pictographs in the front of this desk diary.

For those who are already familiar with the 13-Moon Calendar, this diary is a bridge between the ordinary day planner and the 13-Moon Calendar. For practical reasons, we have decided to work with the week schedule as we know it from the 'ordinary desk diary', starting off on Monday, the first working day. For those who are not familiar with the 13-Moon Calendar, this diary is an easy to use introduction to live the 13 Moon Calendar. We have tried deliberately to keep this desk diary clear, in order to avoid excessive information. This means this desk diary is not complete. The Divine Being of Time is very complex; many books have been written about it. For more detailed information, we would like to refer to those books and to the various websites dedicated to the 13-Moon Calendar. An overview has been included.

All texts have been written by Nicole E. Zonderhuis. They were based on, among others, Mayan-Pleiadian Cosmology by Aluna Joy Yaxk'in and Medicine Cards by Jamie Sams & David Carson. And on personal experiences after living with the 13-Moon Calendar some years.

The Calendar as presented in this desk diary, and from time to time referred to as Tzolkin, is quite different from the Tzolkin or Chol'qui Calendar used by the present-day Mayan shamans. The explanation and names of the seals may be different. Furthermore, the Quiché Maya use a different count. The 13-Moon Calendar as presented in this desk diary is designed by José Argüelles, in order to be used worldwide. It gives everybody the opportunity to get synchronized once again with natural time, and to remember and integrate 'the cycle of 260'.

In Lak'ech,
Nicole E. Zonderhuis and Sylvia Carrilho

Foundation for the Law of Time
& Planet Art Network (PAN)

The mission of the Foundation for the Law of Time is to provide public education concerning the Law of Time and its most practical social application, the 13-Moon 28-day calendar. The Foundation for the Law of Time was especially created (AD 2000) to pace and model the Biosphere-Noosphere transition. As the great shift from historical materialism to the post-historic spiritualization of all of life on Earth, the Biosphere-Noosphere transition is the most significant stage yet in the cycles of terrestrial evolution. Distinguishing between the artificial mechanistic timing frequency (12:60) of global civilization and the natural universal timing frequency (13:20) of the rest of life on Earth, the Law of Time defines the Biosphere-Noosphere transition as a critical 20-year cycle, 1993-2013.

T(E) = Art - The Law of Time
Growing out of a lifetime research by José Argüelles-Valum Votan on the mathematical, prophetic and philosophical principles underlying the Mayan calendar system of Central America, the Law of Time, formulated as T(E) = Art, energy factored by time equals art, demonstrates that time is the universal factor of synchronization, accounting for both the elegance of the natural order and the existence of a universal field of telepathy. The Law of Time so radically alters our notions of time, hitherto based on measurements of space, that it evokes an entirely fresh vision of a transformed world, a world where time is no longer money, but time is art.

13-Moon Calendar and Peace Plan
As the most practical application of the Law of Time, the 13-Moon 28-day calendar is a perpetual and perfectly harmonic standard intended to replace the irregular measure of the present world standard, the Gregorian calendar. Because the implications of such a change are so enormous and so essential for the Biosphere-Noosphere transition, the calendar change is accompanied by a peace plan which promotes peace through culture and a whole system re-envisioning of the role of the human in the Earth's biosphere. To advance the aims of the calendar change peace plan, the Foundation gives support to the Planet Art Network (PAN), a worldwide movement based on the 13-Moon 28-day calendar.

See www.lawoftime.org and www.tortuga.com for more information.

The Banner of Peace

The Banner of Peace is the official flag in use around the world by members of the Planet Art Network and World 13-Moon Calendar Change Peace Movement. It is displayed at all events, gatherings, and centers which promote natural time and planetary peace.

The Roerich Pact and Banner of Peace was designed by Russian artist and humanitarian, Nicholas Roerich (1874 - 1947) as a response to the destruction of the first world war and the Russian Revolution.

It is an international treaty signed by India, the Baltic states, and 22 nations of the Americas including the United States. The Roerich Peace Pact established an international agreement allowing any nation to protect its cultural or artistic heritage with a symbolic banner, the Banner of Peace. Signed in 1935, this treaty is international law today. Just as the Red Cross protects hospitals, the Banner of Peace was implemented to protect culture.
The Pact states, "educational, artistic, and scientific institutions...shall be protected and respected by the belligerents...without any discrimination as to the state allegiance of any particular institution or mission... these missions may display a distinctive flag (the Banner of Peace)...which will entitle them to special protection and respect..." Thus any site of cultural activity around the world can fly the Banner of Peace to declare itself neutral, independent of combatant forces, and protected by international treaty.

The Banner
The distinctive Banner is three red circles surrounded by a larger red circle on a white banner. The deep red color symbolizes the color of our one blood, which is the same for all people. The top circle represents spirituality and encompasses the truth of all religions, that we can all unite regardless of our distinct beliefs. The two circles on the bottom represent art and science. The circle that surrounds the three spheres represents culture, the unity of art, science, and spirituality. The symbol for the Banner of Peace can be found in many cultures and numerous philosophical systems, like on Ethiopian and Coptic antiquities, stone age amulets, Buddhist banners and more. Found in all cultures, the Banner of Peace is the perfect symbol to bring all peoples together in peace.

See www.13moon.com or www.roerich.org for more information.

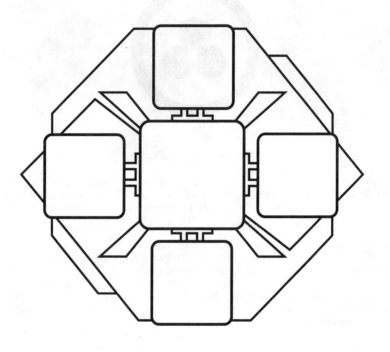

Personal information

Name

Address

City

Phone

E-mail

In case of emergency please notify:

Name

Address

City

Phone

Remaining information:

JANUARY

Mo	Tu	We	Th	Fr	Sa	Su
						1
2	3	4	5	6	7	8
9	10	11	12	13	14	15
16	17	18	19	20	21	22
23	24	25	26	27	28	29
30	31					

FEBRUARY

Mo	Tu	We	Th	Fr	Sa	Su
		1	2	3	4	5
6	7	8	9	10	11	12
13	14	15	16	17	18	19
20	21	22	23	24	25	26
27	28					

MARCH

Mo	Tu	We	Th	Fr	Sa	Su
		1	2	3	4	5
6	7	8	9	10	11	12
13	14	15	16	17	18	19
20	21	22	23	24	25	26
27	28	29	30	31		

APRIL

Mo	Tu	We	Th	Fr	Sa	Su
					1	2
3	4	5	6	7	8	9
10	11	12	13	14	15	16
17	18	19	20	21	22	23
24	25	26	27	28	29	30

MAY

Mo	Tu	We	Th	Fr	Sa	Su
1	2	3	4	5	6	7
8	9	10	11	12	13	14
15	16	17	18	19	20	21
22	23	24	25	26	27	28
29	30	31				

JUNE

Mo	Tu	We	Th	Fr	Sa	Su
			1	2	3	4
5	6	7	8	9	10	11
12	13	14	15	16	17	18
19	20	21	22	23	24	25
26	27	28	29	30		

JULY

Mo	Tu	We	Th	Fr	Sa	Su
					1	2
3	4	5	6	7	8	9
10	11	12	13	14	15	16
17	18	19	20	21	22	23
24	25	26	27	28	29	30
31						

AUGUST

Mo	Tu	We	Th	Fr	Sa	Su
	1	2	3	4	5	6
7	8	9	10	11	12	13
14	15	16	17	18	19	20
21	22	23	24	25	26	27
28	29	30	31			

SEPTEMBER

Mo	Tu	We	Th	Fr	Sa	Su
				1	2	3
4	5	6	7	8	9	10
11	12	13	14	15	16	17
18	19	20	21	22	23	24
25	26	27	28	29	30	

OCTOBER

Mo	Tu	We	Th	Fr	Sa	Su
						1
2	3	4	5	6	7	8
9	10	11	12	13	14	15
16	17	18	19	20	21	22
23	24	25	26	27	28	29
30	31					

NOVEMBER

Mo	Tu	We	Th	Fr	Sa	Su
		1	2	3	4	5
6	7	8	9	10	11	12
13	14	15	16	17	18	19
20	21	22	23	24	25	26
27	28	29	30			

DECEMBER

Mo	Tu	We	Th	Fr	Sa	Su
				1	2	3
4	5	6	7	8	9	10
11	12	13	14	15	16	17
18	19	20	21	22	23	24
25	26	27	28	29	30	31

Jan. 1	New Year's Day
Mar. 20	Spring equinox
	1.26 PM EST - 18.26 GMT
Apr. 14	Good Friday
Apr. 16	Easter Sunday
Apr. 17	Easter Monday
Jun. 21	Summer solstice
	7.26 AM EST - 12.26 GMT
Sep. 22	Autumnal equinox
	11.03 PM EST - 04.03 GMT Sep. 23
Dec. 21	Winter solstice
	7.22 PM EST - 00.22 GMT Dec. 22
Dec. 25	Christmas Day
Dec. 26	Boxing Day

JANUARY

Mo	Tu	We	Th	Fr	Sa	Su
1	2	3	4	5	**6**	**7**
8	9	10	11	12	**13**	**14**
15	16	17	18	19	**20**	**21**
22	23	24	25	26	**27**	**28**
29	30	31				

FEBRUARY

Mo	Tu	We	Th	Fr	Sa	Su
			1	2	**3**	**4**
5	6	7	8	9	**10**	**11**
12	13	14	15	16	**17**	**18**
19	20	21	22	23	**24**	**25**
26	27	28				

MARCH

Mo	Tu	We	Th	Fr	Sa	Su
			1	2	**3**	**4**
5	6	7	8	9	**10**	**11**
12	13	14	15	16	**17**	**18**
19	20	21	22	23	**24**	**25**
26	27	28	29	30	**31**	

APRIL

Mo	Tu	We	Th	Fr	Sa	Su
						1
2	3	4	5	6	**7**	**8**
9	10	11	12	13	**14**	**15**
16	17	18	19	20	**21**	**22**
23	24	25	26	27	**28**	**29**
30						

MAY

Mo	Tu	We	Th	Fr	Sa	Su
	1	2	3	4	**5**	**6**
7	8	9	10	11	**12**	**13**
14	15	16	17	18	**19**	**20**
21	22	23	24	25	**26**	**27**
28	29	30	31			

JUNE

Mo	Tu	We	Th	Fr	Sa	Su
				1	**2**	**3**
4	5	6	7	8	**9**	**10**
11	12	13	14	15	**16**	**17**
18	19	20	21	22	**23**	**24**
25	26	27	28	29	**30**	

JULY

Mo	Tu	We	Th	Fr	Sa	Su
						1
2	3	4	5	6	**7**	**8**
9	10	11	12	13	**14**	**15**
16	17	18	19	20	**21**	**22**
23	24	25	26	27	**28**	**29**
30	31					

AUGUST

Mo	Tu	We	Th	Fr	Sa	Su
		1	2	3	**4**	**5**
6	7	8	9	10	**11**	**12**
13	14	15	16	17	**18**	**19**
20	21	22	23	24	**25**	**26**
27	28	29	30	**31**		

SEPTEMBER

Mo	Tu	We	Th	Fr	Sa	Su
					1	**2**
3	4	5	6	7	**8**	**9**
10	11	12	13	14	**15**	**16**
17	18	19	20	21	**22**	**23**
24	25	26	27	28	**29**	**30**

OCTOBER

Mo	Tu	We	Th	Fr	Sa	Su
1	2	3	4	5	**6**	**7**
8	9	10	11	12	**13**	**14**
15	16	17	18	19	**20**	**21**
22	23	24	25	26	**27**	**28**
29	30	31				

NOVEMBER

Mo	Tu	We	Th	Fr	Sa	Su
			1	2	**3**	**4**
5	6	7	8	9	**10**	**11**
12	13	14	15	16	**17**	**18**
19	20	21	22	23	**24**	**25**
26	27	28	29	30		

DECEMBER

Mo	Tu	We	Th	Fr	Sa	Su
					1	**2**
3	4	5	6	7	**8**	**9**
10	11	12	13	14	**15**	**16**
17	18	19	20	21	**22**	**23**
24	25	26	27	28	**29**	**30**
31						

Jan. 1	New Year's Day
Mar. 20	Spring equinox
	7.07 PM EST - 00.07 GMT Mar. 21
Apr. 6	Good Friday
Apr. 8	Easter Sunday
Apr. 9	Easter Monday
Jun. 21	Summer solstice
	1.06 PM EST - 18.06 GMT

Sep. 23	Autumnal equinox
	4.51 AM EST - 09.51 GMT
Dec. 22	Winter solstice
	1.08 AM EST - 06.08 GMT
Dec. 25	Christmas Day
Dec. 26	Boxing Day

School/work time-table

This universal time-table can be easily adjusted for school or work and can be used as a weekly or monthly overview.

WHEN	WHAT	WHO	WHERE

WHEN	WHAT	WHO	WHERE

WHEN	WHAT	WHO	WHERE

WHEN	WHAT	WHO	WHERE

WHEN	WHAT	WHO	WHERE

WHEN	WHAT	WHO	WHERE

WHEN	WHAT	WHO	WHERE

School/work time-table

WHEN	WHAT	WHO	WHERE

WHEN	WHAT	WHO	WHERE

WHEN	WHAT	WHO	WHERE

WHEN	WHAT	WHO	WHERE

WHEN	WHAT	WHO	WHERE

WHEN	WHAT	WHO	WHERE

WHEN	WHAT	WHO	WHERE

WHEN	WHAT	WHO	WHERE

Moonplanner
Yellow Cosmic Seed Year

1/10	**1**	2/7
1/11	**2**	2/8
1/12	**3**	2/9
1/13	**4**	2/10
1/14	**5**	2/11
1/15	**6**	2/12
1/16	**7**	2/13
1/17	**8**	2/14
1/18	**9**	2/15
1/19	**10**	2/16
1/20	**11**	2/17
1/21	**12**	2/18
1/22	**13**	2/19
1/23	**14**	2/20
1/24	**15**	2/21
1/25	**16**	2/22
1/26	**17**	2/23
1/27	**18**	2/24
1/28	**19**	2/25
1/29	**20**	2/26
1/30	**21**	2/27
1/31	**22**	2/28
2/1	**23**	3/1
2/2	**24**	3/2
2/3	**25**	3/3
2/4	**26**	3/4
2/5	**27**	3/5
2/6	**28**	3/6

Moonplanner
Yellow Cosmic Seed Year

3/7	**1**	4/4
3/8	**2** ☽	4/5
3/9	**3**	4/6
3/10	**4**	4/7
3/11	**5**	4/8
3/12	**6**	4/9
3/13	**7**	4/10
3/14	⊕ **8**	4/11
3/15	**9**	4/12
3/16	**10** ⊕	4/13
3/17	**11**	4/14
3/18	**12**	4/15
3/19	**13**	4/16
3/20	**14**	4/17
3/21	**15**	4/18
3/22	◑ **16**	4/19
3/23	**17**	4/20
3/24	**18** ◑	4/21
3/25	**19**	4/22
3/26	**20**	4/23
3/27	**21**	4/24
3/28	**22**	4/25
3/29	● **23**	4/26
3/30	**24** ●	4/27
3/31	**25**	4/28
4/1	**26**	4/29
4/2	**27**	4/30
4/3	**28**	5/1

MAY 2 - MAY 29
2006

Moonplanner
Yellow Cosmic Seed Year

MAY 30 - JUN 26
2006

5/2	**1**		5/30
5/3	**2**		5/31
5/4	**3**		6/1
5/5	◐ **4**		6/2
5/6	**5** ◐		6/3
5/7	**6**		6/4
5/8	**7**		6/5
5/9	**8**		6/6
5/10	**9**		6/7
5/11	**10**		6/8
5/12	**11**		6/9
5/13	⊕ **12**		6/10
5/14	**13** ⊕		6/11
5/15	**14**		6/12
5/16	**15**		6/13
5/17	**16**		6/14
5/18	**17**		6/15
5/19	**18**		6/16
5/20	◑ **19**		6/17
5/21	**20** ◑		6/18
5/22	**21**		6/19
5/23	**22**		6/20
5/24	**23**		6/21
5/25	**24**		6/22
5/26	**25**		6/23
5/27	● **26**		6/24
5/28	**27** ●		6/25
5/29	**28**		6/26

JUN 27 - JUL 24
2006

Moonplanner

*Yellow Cosmic
Seed Year*

*Red Magnetic
Moon Year*

JUL 26 - AUG 22
2006

6/27	*1*	7/26
6/28	*2*	7/27
6/29	*3*	7/28
6/30	*4*	7/29
7/1	*5*	7/30
7/2	*6*	7/31
7/3	◑ *7*	8/1
7/4	*8* ◑	8/2
7/5	*9*	8/3
7/6	*10*	8/4
7/7	*11*	8/5
7/8	*12*	8/6
7/9	*13*	8/7
7/10	*14*	8/8
7/11	○ *15* ○	8/9
7/12	*16*	8/10
7/13	*17*	8/11
7/14	*18*	8/12
7/15	*19*	8/13
7/16	*20*	8/14
7/17	◐ *21*	8/15
7/18	*22* ◐	8/16
7/19	*23*	8/17
7/20	*24*	8/18
7/21	*25*	8/19
7/22	*26*	8/20
7/23	*27*	8/21
7/24	*28*	8/22

7/25 *Day out of Time* ●

AUG 23 - SEP 19
2006

Moonplanner
Red Magnetic Moon Year

SEP 20 - OCT 17
2006

8/23	1	9/20
8/24	2	9/21
8/25	3	9/22
8/26	4	9/23
8/27	5	9/24
8/28	6	9/25
8/29	7	9/26
8/30	8	9/27
8/31	9	9/28
9/1	10	9/29
9/2	11	9/30
9/3	12	10/1
9/4	13	10/2
9/5	14	10/3
9/6	15	10/4
9/7	16	10/5
9/8	17	10/6
9/9	18	10/7
9/10	19	10/8
9/11	20	10/9
9/12	21	10/10
9/13	22	10/11
9/14	23	10/12
9/15	24	10/13
9/16	25	10/14
9/17	26	10/15
9/18	27	10/16
9/19	28	10/17

Moonplanner
Red Magnetic Moon Year

10/18	*1*	11/15
10/19	*2*	11/16
10/20	*3*	11/17
10/21	*4*	11/18
10/22	☽ *5*	11/19
10/23	*6* ☽	11/20
10/24	*7*	11/21
10/25	*8*	11/22
10/26	*9*	11/23
10/27	*10*	11/24
10/28	*11*	11/25
10/29	☽ *12*	11/26
10/30	*13*	11/27
10/31	*14* ☽	11/28
11/1	*15*	11/29
11/2	*16*	11/30
11/3	*17*	12/1
11/4	*18*	12/2
11/5	☽ *19*	12/3
11/6	*20*	12/4
11/7	*21* ☽	12/5
11/8	*22*	12/6
11/9	*23*	12/7
11/10	*24*	12/8
11/11	*25*	12/9
11/12	☽ *26*	12/10
11/13	*27*	12/11
11/14	*28* ☽	12/12

DEC 13 - JAN 9
2006 / 2007

Moonplanner
Red Magnetic Moon Year

JAN 10 - FEB 6
2007

12/13	**1**		1/10
12/14	**2** ◑		1/11
12/15	**3**		1/12
12/16	**4**		1/13
12/17	**5**		1/14
12/18	**6**		1/15
12/19	**7**		1/16
12/20	◑ **8**		1/17
12/21	**9**		1/18
12/22	**10** ●		1/19
12/23	**11**		1/20
12/24	**12**		1/21
12/25	**13**		1/22
12/26	**14**		1/23
12/27	◐ **15**		1/24
12/28	**16** ◐		1/25
12/29	**17**		1/26
12/30	**18**		1/27
12/31	**19**		1/28
1/1	**20**		1/29
1/2	**21**		1/30
1/3	◯ **22**		1/31
1/4	**23**		2/1
1/5	**24** ◯		2/2
1/6	**25**		2/3
1/7	**26**		2/4
1/8	**27**		2/5
1/9	**28**		2/6

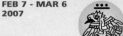

Moonplanner
Red Magnetic Moon Year

2/7	**1**	3/7
2/8	**2**	3/8
2/9	**3**	3/9
2/10	◑ **4**	3/10
2/11	**5**	3/11
2/12	**6** ◐	3/12
2/13	**7**	3/13
2/14	**8**	3/14
2/15	**9**	3/15
2/16	**10**	3/16
2/17	● **11**	3/17
2/18	**12**	3/18
2/19	**13** ●	3/19
2/20	**14**	3/20
2/21	**15**	3/21
2/22	**16**	3/22
2/23	**17**	3/23
2/24	◐ **18**	3/24
2/25	**19** ◐	3/25
2/26	**20**	3/26
2/27	**21**	3/27
2/28	**22**	3/28
3/1	**23**	3/29
3/2	**24**	3/30
3/3	◯ **25**	3/31
3/4	**26**	4/1
3/5	**27** ◯	4/2
3/6	**28**	4/3

APR 4 - MAY 1
2007

Moonplanner
Red Magnetic Moon Year

MAY 2 - MAY 29
2007

4/4	*1*	5/2
4/5	*2*	5/3
4/6	*3*	5/4
4/7	*4*	5/5
4/8	*5*	5/6
4/9	*6*	5/7
4/10	*7*	5/8
4/11	*8*	5/9
4/12	*9*	5/10
4/13	*10*	5/11
4/14	*11*	5/12
4/15	*12*	5/13
4/16	*13*	5/14
4/17	*14*	5/15
4/18	*15*	5/16
4/19	*16*	5/17
4/20	*17*	5/18
4/21	*18*	5/19
4/22	*19*	5/20
4/23	*20*	5/21
4/24	*21*	5/22
4/25	*22*	5/23
4/26	*23*	5/24
4/27	*24*	5/25
4/28	*25*	5/26
4/29	*26*	5/27
4/30	*27*	5/28
5/1	*28*	5/29

Moonplanner
Red Magnetic Moon Year

5/30	*1*	6/27
5/31	*2*	6/28
6/1	☽ *3*	6/29
6/2	*4* ☽	6/30
6/3	*5*	7/1
6/4	*6*	7/2
6/5	*7*	7/3
6/6	*8*	7/4
6/7	*9*	7/5
6/8	◑ *10*	7/6
6/9	*11* ◑	7/7
6/10	*12*	7/8
6/11	*13*	7/9
6/12	*14*	7/10
6/13	*15*	7/11
6/14	*16*	7/12
6/15	● *17*	7/13
6/16	*18* ●	7/14
6/17	*19*	7/15
6/18	*20*	7/16
6/19	*21*	7/17
6/20	*22*	7/18
6/21	*23*	7/19
6/22	◐ *24*	7/20
6/23	*25*	7/21
6/24	*26* ◐	7/22
6/25	*27*	7/23
6/26	*28*	7/24

Day out of Time 7/25

This calendar can be used to develop an overview of cycles in your body. And of course to check if and what kind of cycles there are in your body and mind. You can use different colors and/or symbols to mark different cycles.

Example: happy/sad feelings, stressed or sexy! And menstruation, ovulation or a headache.

The days in this calendar are marked with the Kin number of the Tzolkin.

1. Check the Kin number of the first day of your cycle. Example: January 20, 2006 = Kin 22 (9 Wind)

2. Mark the found Kin number on the Cycle Calendar.

3. After several Moons the rhythm of your cycle(s) will be shown.

Examples:

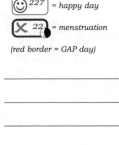

☺ 227 = happy day

✗ 22 = menstruation

(red border = GAP day)

_____
_____
_____
_____
_____
_____
_____

#	•	••	•••	••••	—
1	104	132	160	188	216
2	105	133	161	189	217
3	106	134	162	190	218
4	107	135	163	191	219
5	108	136	164	192	220
6	109	137	165	193	221
7	110	138	166	194	222
8	111	139	167	195	223
9	112	140	168	196	224
10	113	141	169	197	225
11	114	142	170	198	226
12	115	143	171	199	227
13	116	144	172	200	228
14	117	145	173	201	229
15	118	146	174	202	230
16	119	147	175	203	231
17	120	148	176	204	232
18	121	149	177	205	233
19	122	150	178	206	234
20	123	151	179	207	235
21	124	152	180	208	236
22	125	153	181	209	237
23	126	154	182	210	238
24	127	155	183	211	239
25	128	156	184	212	240
26	129	157	185	213	241
27	130	158	186	214	242
28	131	159	187	215	243

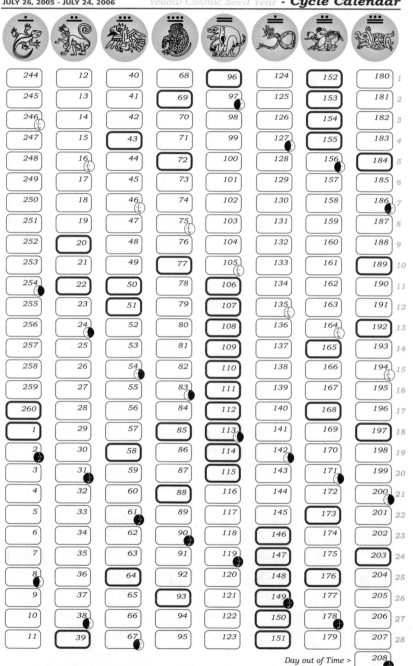

244	12	40	68	96	124	152	180	1
245	13	41	69	97	125	153	181	2
246	14	42	70	98	126	154	182	3
247	15	43	71	99	127	155	183	4
248	16	44	72	100	128	156	184	5
249	17	45	73	101	129	157	185	6
250	18	46	74	102	130	158	186	7
251	19	47	75	103	131	159	187	8
252	20	48	76	104	132	160	188	9
253	21	49	77	105	133	161	189	10
254	22	50	78	106	134	162	190	11
255	23	51	79	107	135	163	191	12
256	24	52	80	108	136	164	192	13
257	25	53	81	109	137	165	193	14
258	26	54	82	110	138	166	194	15
259	27	55	83	111	139	167	195	16
260	28	56	84	112	140	168	196	17
1	29	57	85	113	141	169	197	18
2	30	58	86	114	142	170	198	19
3	31	59	87	115	143	171	199	20
4	32	60	88	116	144	172	200	21
5	33	61	89	117	145	173	201	22
6	34	62	90	118	146	174	202	23
7	35	63	91	119	147	175	203	24
8	36	64	92	120	148	176	204	25
9	37	65	93	121	149	177	205	26
10	38	66	94	122	150	178	206	27
11	39	67	95	123	151	179	207	28

Day out of Time > 208

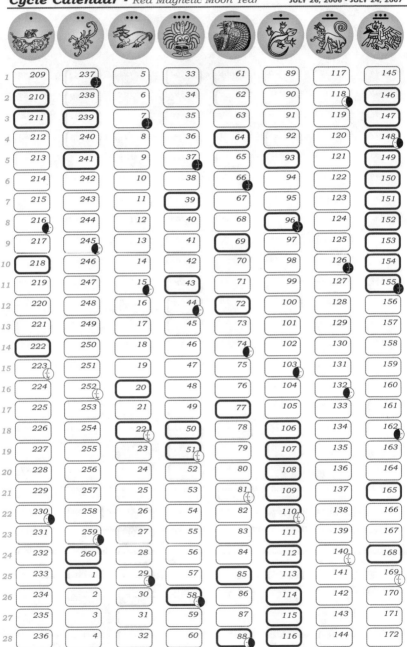

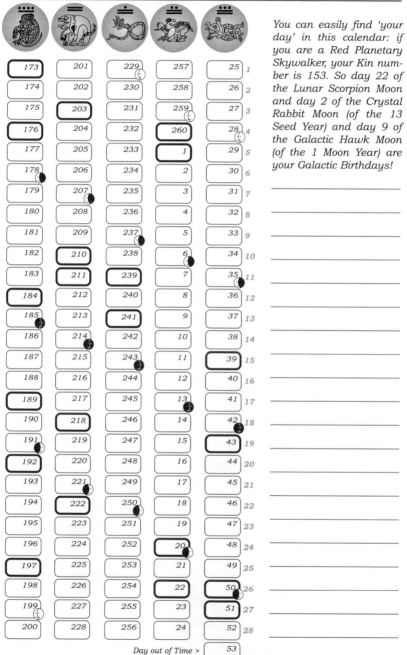

You can easily find 'your day' in this calendar: if you are a Red Planetary Skywalker, your Kin number is 153. So day 22 of the Lunar Scorpion Moon and day 2 of the Crystal Rabbit Moon (of the 13 Seed Year) and day 9 of the Galactic Hawk Moon (of the 1 Moon Year) are your Galactic Birthdays!

173	201	229	257	25	1
174	202	230	258	26	2
175	203	231	259	27	3
176	204	232	260	28	4
177	205	233	1	29	5
178	206	234	2	30	6
179	207	235	3	31	7
180	208	236	4	32	8
181	209	237	5	33	9
182	210	238	6	34	10
183	211	239	7	35	11
184	212	240	8	36	12
185	213	241	9	37	13
186	214	242	10	38	14
187	215	243	11	39	15
188	216	244	12	40	16
189	217	245	13	41	17
190	218	246	14	42	18
191	219	247	15	43	19
192	220	248	16	44	20
193	221	249	17	45	21
194	222	250	18	46	22
195	223	251	19	47	23
196	224	252	20	48	24
197	225	253	21	49	25
198	226	254	22	50	26
199	227	255	23	51	27
200	228	256	24	52	28
			Day out of Time >	53	

Notes

Notes

This is the first year in which this diary is in use. Therefore, we would like to ask everybody to provide us with tips and remarks about its usage. What information do you miss? What is not clear, what is excessive? And what is your experience with the Seals and the days?
Please send us an e-mail to: info@mayatzolkin.com

Visit www.mayatzolkin.com for tips and updates.

Mayan priest wearing a jaquar pelt. (Temple of the Cross in Palenque)

Now is the time to remember

The fact that you bought this diary, means that you remember… each day is different. Some days are better for a specific activity than others. That's why you need your desk diary: so you can plan. And when you plan, you probably take into account all sorts of practical circumstances. Quite likely, you have noticed that some days turned out to be perfect for a specific activity. As if it were no coincidence that you picked this day in the first place. And you know what? It wasn't!

The 13-Moon Calendar contains one year of 365 days, combined with a 260-day calendar. The source of these calendars is Mayan. They called the annual calendar the Haab and the 260-day cycle the Tzolkin. The ancient Mayan culture of Yucatán was very advanced in its knowledge of the time cycles. They knew things that we only discovered recently by means of modern technology. It seems the Maya were able to look at our solar system from above. The calendar they designed is the most accurate calendar in the world. Not once did it have to be adjusted, contrary to our Gregorian Calendar. The 12-month Gregorian calendar is not only inaccurate, it is also "arbitrary and irregular, lacking any correspondence to actual cycles of nature. Some of the months are 31 days, some 30, yet February gets 28 days, except for an extra day once every four years (but not on centuries, except those divisible by the number four). The 12-month calendar hides the 13th moon. The number 13 is now surrounded by superstition and is considered taboo; unlucky and/or evil. This fear is reinforced by cultural antiquities like 'Friday the thirteenth'. Often buildings have no 13th floor, or avoid constructing a number 13 apt unit. Why? The ancient Maya had an entirely different relationship to the number 13, actually revering it as the Key to Time itself. 13 is the Mayan galactic prime number; the Force of The Universal Movement of Creation." (Quotation: Eden Sky.) Together with number 20 it is the base for the Tzolkin Calendar.

The Tzolkin Calendar contributes a specific energy to each day. This is precisely what many people feel: every day is different, even if you plan, fill and spend them in exactly the same way. This desk diary offers you the possibility to attune to this energy. For instance, it might be wise not to make important decisions on a Moon seal day, since feelings and emotions dominate during those days. During Wizard days it's wise to plan strictly, for those are the days when timelessness dominates and the hours pass unnoticed.

It is hard to fully understand the meaning of all information at once. But it is important to see that there is another calendar which gives everybody the opportunity to get synchronized once again with natural time, and to remember 'the cycle of 260'. Don't try too hard to understand it all. After all, there are 260 different combinations. Use the words are as threads by which the image of the energy forms. You may just suddenly recognize the features of the energy in a day, a year or a person. It will come to you. All you have to do is remember…

This image is indicating important information.
Like 'Remember' or 'Store in your shell!'.

On January 1, in many countries all over the world people celebrate New Year: a new start with new chances and good resolutions. This calls for a new and empty diary! However, only few people are aware of the fact that this magical date - January 1 - is based on an agreement that we once made. The duration of a year is based on the time needed for our planet to go around the Sun. After 365 ¼ days we are back at where we started. But there are no marks on this orbit that indicate the beginning or the end. In other words, our year could very well start off on another date. It simply depends on the date we agree upon...

The ancient Maya and Egyptians agreed upon a different date: their year started on July 26. They were aware of the fact that on July 26, the Sun and Sirius both arise at our horizon at exactly the same moment and exactly the same place. With only a minor difference of 3 minutes, the Earth, Sun and Sirius are aligned on that moment. No other synchronicity between those 3 heavenly bodies occurs throughout the year. That's why the 13-Moon Calendar starts on July 26. So no happy New Year; the year has already half gone! We now live in the year of the Yellow Cosmic Seed. The year is called after the Tone and Seal of the first day of the year. See page 69 for the year energy.

  Remember: July 26 is the first day of the new year.

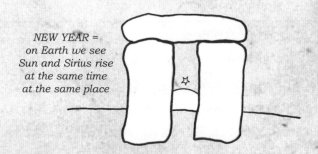

NEW YEAR =
on Earth we see
Sun and Sirius rise
at the same time
at the same place

13-Moon Calendar

Our month has everything to do with the Moon. The orbit of the Moon around the Earth consists of 4 phases of 7. We know:

🌑 *New Moon*

🌓 *First Quarter*

🌕 *Full Moon*

🌗 *Last Quarter*

> 👣 *In the old mayan codices you can find these kind of footsteps to indicate the chronology of the story: read the picture and follow the footsteps to the next picture. In this diary the footsteps also indicate that the text is continued on the next page.*

These phases form the basis of our week. The time between two Full Moons once determined our month. Since the Earth also turns around itself, it seems to take 29 ½ days to get from one Full Moon to the next. But did you know that the Moon orbits our Earth precisely 13 times, when we orbit the Sun just once? You could see this very clearly if you would look down on our solar system. That's why the 13-Moon Calendar consists of 13 months/Moons of each 28 days. So a year is 13 x 28 = 364 days. The day that remains is called the Day Out of Time. It is the day between the years. It is a holiday of connections; the old is released and the intention for the new year is set. Each year the Day out of Time is celebrated on July 25.

1st Moon	**Bat Moon**	*July 26 - August 22*
2nd Moon	**Scorpion Moon**	*August 23 - September 19*
3rd Moon	**Deer Moon**	*September 20 - October 17*
4th Moon	**Owl Moon**	*October 18 - November 14*
5th Moon	**Peacock Moon**	*November 15 - December 12*
6th Moon	**Lizard Moon**	*December 13 - January 9*
7th Moon	**Monkey Moon**	*January 10 - February 6*
8th Moon	**Hawk Moon**	*February 7 - March 6*
9th Moon	**Jaguar Moon**	*March 7 - April 3*
10th Moon	**Dog Moon**	*April 4 - May 1*
11th Moon	**Serpent Moon**	*May 2 - May 29*
12th Moon	**Rabbit Moon**	*May 30 - June 26*
13th Moon	**Turtle Moon**	*June 27 - July 24*

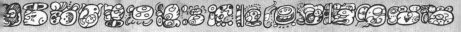

In the 13-Moon Calendar each Moon has its own totem animal (see tabel).
The sequence of the 13 Moons with their totem animals is also pure Mayan and
corresponds to the sequence of thirteen Mayan constellations as re-discovered
and presented by Hugh Harleston in El Zodiaco Maya (1991).

José Argüelles wrote a wonderful story about Time, in which Turtle and Tree
were appointed Keepers of Time by grandmother Milky Way. Turtle travelled to
the Moon (chapter 14) and met 12 animals, each sitting in a small lodge on the
Moon. The last lodge was empty, obviously meant and waiting for Turtle. You
can find this story on www.tortuga.com.

We can discover more about the meaning and energy of the 13 Moons, by
studying the characteristics of the animals. During the year at the beginning
of each Moon/month you will find this specific information.

Remember: one year consists of 13 Moons/month.

Year Wavespell

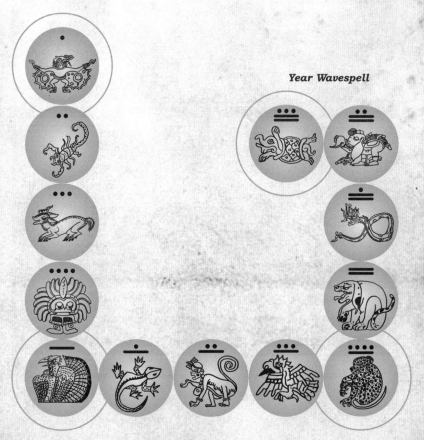

Galactic Calendar (Tzolkin)

Dragon	1	21	41	61	81	101	121	141	161	181	201	221	241
Wind	2	22	42	62	82	102	122	142	162	182	202	222	242
Night	3	23	43	63	83	103	123	143	163	183	203	223	243
Seed	4	24	44	64	84	104	124	144	164	184	204	224	244
Serpent	5	25	45	65	85	105	125	145	165	185	205	225	245
World Bridger	6	26	46	66	86	106	126	146	166	186	206	226	246
Hand	7	27	47	67	87	107	127	147	167	187	207	227	247
Star	8	28	48	68	88	108	128	148	168	188	208	228	248
Moon	9	29	49	69	89	109	129	149	169	189	209	229	249
Dog	10	30	50	70	90	110	130	150	170	190	210	230	250
Monkey	11	31	51	71	91	111	131	151	171	191	211	231	251
Human	12	32	52	72	92	112	132	152	172	192	212	232	252
Sky Walker	13	33	53	73	93	113	133	153	173	193	213	233	253
Wizard	14	34	54	74	94	114	134	154	174	194	214	234	254
Eagle	15	35	55	75	95	115	135	155	175	195	215	235	255
Warrior	16	36	56	76	96	116	136	156	176	196	216	236	256
Earth	17	37	57	77	97	117	137	157	177	197	217	237	257
Mirror	18	38	58	78	98	118	138	158	178	198	218	238	258
Storm	19	39	59	79	99	119	139	159	179	199	219	239	259
Sun	20	40	60	80	100	120	140	160	180	200	220	240	260

Galactic Calendar (Tzolkin)

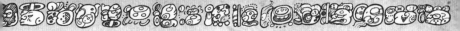

The Galactic Calendar is based on the Tzolkin, the sacred 260-day calendar of the Maya. This calendar has been attuned to the natural cycles of the human body and to the cycle of the Earth, the Moon and the Sun, but also to the cycle of the Earth and the stargroup the Pleiades and the entire Milky Way. That's why we call it the Galactic Calendar, named after Galaxis, the Milky Way. The ancient Maya knew what we have only just rediscovered; our Earth has 3 orbits:
1) Earth turns around its own axis in 24 hours
2) Earth orbits the Sun in one year
3) together with our Sun, Earth orbits Alcyone, the central sun of the Pleiades.

This last one is called the Precessional Cycle of approximately 26.000 years. The 260-day Tzolkin is a fractal of this cycle, a part that contains all character-istics of the entire Precessional Cycle. For the ancient Maya, the relationship with the Milky Way was part of their every day reality. And not only that. We too are familiar with this 260-day cycle from the early start of our life, as the average human pregnancy lasts 260 days. It takes 260 days for a human ovum and sperm-cell to evolve into a complete human being, ready to be born. So it really is very weird that we have forgotten all about this 260-day cycle. Yet, we may very well carry the recollection of this 9-month cycle in our body.

Recently, my friend's baby got very ill, precisely 260 days after his birth. The doctors had no idea what was going on. Perhaps the baby relived his birth. Just before being born, babies start feeling oppressed and want to get out. The baby might have felt this energy again 260 days after. If so, it is advisable to give extra love and attention around this time, it could heal possible birth trauma.

260 and 365 days?
The 260-day calendar and the 365-day calendar exist simultaneously. Try to imagine them as two wheels: one with 260 teeth and the other with 365 teeth. When the 260-wheel (Tzolkin) has turned around once, the 365-wheel (1 year) still has 105 teeth to go. After 52 years the first day of the Tzolkin coincides with the first day of the Annual Calendar. In other words: after 52 years you celebrate your birthday with the same seal as on the day you were born. The Maya called a 52 year old an 'elder'.

13 : 20
The 260 days of the Galactic Calendar consist of 13 Tones and 20 Solar Seals. This gives us 13 x 20 combinations = 260. There are 13 Tones, each one marked as a dot-bar notation. The Solar Seals carry names as Dragon, Wind, Night, Seed, Warrior, Monkey, etc. Each combination is called a 'kin'. The kin is the smallest possible particle that still carries all characteristics of creation: a day is a kin, but you too as a human being are a kin, since you are indivisible. A kin can be, for instance, 8 Dragon, or 11 Warrior. Every kin has its own energy and its own function. The frequency of the 13-Moon Calendar is 13 : 20, contrary to the 12 : 60 - our regulated time of 60 mechanical minutes and 2 x 12 hours.

The Tzolkin gives you the energy of each individual day. By living by this calendar, you can get attuned to Hunab K'u, the very heart of our Milky Way. And once you are attuned to the natural cycles, things will occur that you would previously have considered coincidence. That's when you know that you are on the right frequency...

Galactic Calendar (Tzolkin)

🔴 **Red - white - blue - yellow = the cycle of 4**

The smallest cycle that can be found everywhere in the 13-Moon Calendar is 4 (red, white, blue, yellow), determined by the 4 directions of the wind. We always start in the East. Every direction has its own color and quality or power. Every day, both the seals and the weeks and months change color. We call a cycle of 4 a Harmonic or a Time Cell. See Moon 1 for an example of how to work with this energy.

East	color red	power of initiation
North	color white	power of refinement
West	color blue	power of transformation
South	color yellow	power of ripening

When you take a look in the journal at the weeks of the Moons, you will see that each week has its own color. (Colored lines above the days.) You can use this every Moon. Each Moon has 4 phases: 4 weeks of 7 days. The first week's color is red: good for initiation. The second week's color is white: good for refinement, etc.

lak'in	xaman	chik'in	nohol
(east)	(north)	(west)	(south)

Galactic Activation Portals - GAP

The Galactic Calendar, or Tzolkin, has 52 dark (or black) sections. These are the so-called Galactic Activation Portal days (GAPs). This 52-day pattern is called 'the Loom of Maya'. During the GAPs, the veils between the visible and invisible world are thinner. That's when we are more intensely connected with Hunab K'u, the heart of the Milky Way, the Source. Some people notice they can meditate better on a GAP-day, some have a stronger focus within. A GAP may seem to women as the Moontime or menstruation: there seems to be a thin layer between you and the world around you, your focus is more within than usual. At the same time, the connection with above and below - the Earth - is stronger. For me personally, I try to stay indoors as much as I can when I menstruate on a GAP-day, because the pace of the outside world is just too much for me during those days, whereas beautiful and creative things may be born in the peace and quiet of my home.

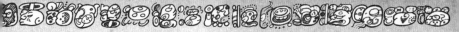

Core Days

The Core Days can be found in the center column, the 7th colomn, of the Tzolkin, from Kin 121 onward: Red Self-Existing Dragon (4 Imix) up to and including Yellow Planetary Sun (10 Ahau). It is the central column in the Tzolkin, the spine. It is also called the mystic column. This 20-day time period definitely conveys the power of the number 7: channeling, mystic power, resonance, attunement. During those days, the energy is strongly focused on the Here and Now; this can be experienced quite intensely. It is wise to keep your attention focused on your self, instead of on past and future. The Core Days can helps us concentrate on the Here and Now.

The Present-Day Maya

The Galactic Calendar as presented in this diary, and from time to time referred to as Tzolkin, is quite different from the Tzolkin or Chol'qui Calendar used by the present-day Mayan shamans. The explanation and names of the Seals may be different. Furthermore, the Quiché Maya use a different count. The 13-Moon Calendar as presented in this diary is designed by José Argüelles, in order to be used world-wide. It gives everybody the opportunity to get synchronized once again with natural time, and to remember and integrate 'the cycle of 260'.

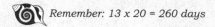

Remember: 13 x 20 = 260 days

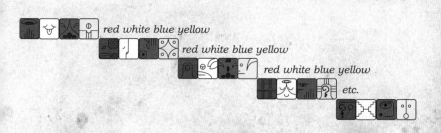

red white blue yellow

red white blue yellow

red white blue yellow

etc.

Wavespell

Do you often have too little time in a week to finish a project? For many people, the 5-day working week passes by too fast. If you share that experience, the Galactic Calendar might come as a solution: it contains a 13-day week. We call this week a Wavespell. Whether you like it or not, time goes by, like the waves keep on undulating.

"You can learn how to stop the waves. But you can also learn how to surf."
- Joseph Goldstein -

And that's exactly where we find the secret of 'having time'. If you have know-ledge of time, you can surf on that undulation, which saves a lot of energy! You'll be surfing the Wavespell. A Wavespell is like a large undulation, divided into 13 steps. Try to visualize a wave. As if by magic, the water is being pushed forward, it rises and rises, the wave becomes bigger and bigger, until it collapses under its own weight and breaks. It dissolves in the sea and all that is left of its existence is a little foam. You can divide this movement into several phases, like the 13-Tone Wavespell in the table below.

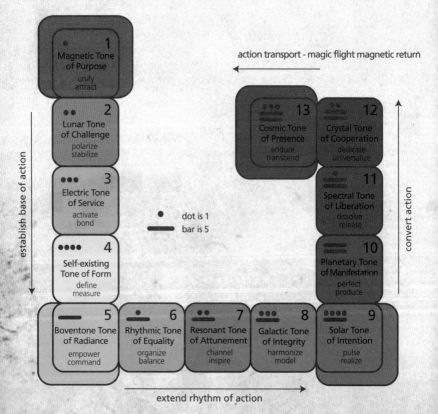

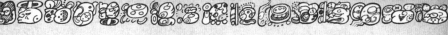

In the first phase (1-4), energy (water) is being collected below the water surface. Above the water surface there is nothing that indicates the rising of a wave. This is what we call 'establish basis for action', or 'the organization of energy'. Then (at 5) the water rises. The wave can now be seen above the water surface and it keeps rising until 9. The wave reaches its highest point at 10 and breaks. What was built up in the previous steps, now falls apart or disperses (10-12). The water spreads until the surface is smooth again (13). It is a moment of silence. The wave may now be born again, and it may not. That is its magic.

We call the corner points of the Wavespell the Towers (Tone 1, 5, 9 and 13). This is where a change of direction of the process of creation takes place. It is a magical point, since this change seems to occur without any visible intervention. It is the intervention of the fourth dimension: the pulsar of Time.

This process of 13 steps can be found in everything, both on a large scale and in small processes. The Wavespell is a fractal: it is a series of 13 days, a year with 13-Moons, but also a series of 13 years. A series of 13 can finish a process of creation. After the magical flight of Tone 13, you go to a new beginning at Tone 1. This may be a higher level of the same process of creation.

Take a look at the following summery of how you can finish a project in 13 steps:

1.	Attract energy	Define purpose
2.	Stabilize energy	Define challenge
3.	Bond energy	Describe demand of target group
4.	Measure energy	Define requirements
5.	Command energy	Collect means
6.	Balance energy	Organize means, locate
7.	Inspire energy	Adjust team, production
8.	Model energy	Action takes shape
9.	Realize energy	Produce
10.	Produce energy	Manifestation of product/service - presentation
11.	Release energy	Go marketing
12.	Universalize energy	Meet and evaluate process
13.	Magical flight	Rest and preparation for the next process

Practical

The Galactic Calendar has 20 Wavespells: 20 x a series of 13 Tones (= 260). A Wavespell starts with a Tone 1-Kin.

Top left in the Galactic Calendar you can find the first Wavespell: the (Red) Dragon Wavespell. The second Wavespell starts 13 kins later; the (White) Wizard Wavespell. Then there is the (Blue) Hand Wavespell and then the (Yellow) Sun Wavespell. Once again we see the cycle of the 4 colors (first red, then white, blue and yellow). Even when you have no knowledge whatsoever of the existence of the Wavespells, they are there. Just like the seasons of the year. The first day of a Wavespell is important, because it gives its energy to the entire series. The characteristics of the Seal influence the next 13 days. For instance, a Wind Wavespell can be characterized by the key words Communication - Breath - Spirit. During these 13 days, it is wise to pay extra attention to communication, in order not to misunderstand one another. The Wavespells will be explained with the Moon energies later.

Tones

The 13 Tones are 13 sacred numbers, spiritual energies - beyond physical reality - that give us the power to create. Each Tone has the numerical significance of the number itself, but it is also related to the other Tones. After all, it is just one step in the Wavespell. The Tone indicates the energy you can use on any given day. It is like the blowing wind: with the wind in your back it is so much easier to cycle...

The Tones are expressed as dot-bar notations. This way of expressing numbers goes all the way back to the ancient Maya and is quite simple. Each dot is 1, 5 dots are presented as a bar, 5 fingers are one hand. So, 1 bar and 1 dot form number 6.

Each Tone has its own name and is named after the type of energy it represents. Furthermore, each Tone has its own key words that you can find in the table.

Tone 1
Magnetic Tone of Purpose
Attract Energy - Receive!

Visualize a dot on an empty sheet of paper. All you can do is stare at the dot. It attracts you like a magnet. That is why this is the Magnetic Tone. We are at the beginning of a series of 13, so this Tone is good for setting a purpose and to collect energy. Receive it!

Features: *people with Tone 1 tend to be bold. They do not like routine. They are good at bringing together people/means and at initiating projects. However, finishing those projects is not their strongest quality. They like to be in the center of attention and tend to have their own opinion about things. They might 'forget' to receive the good things they attract.*

Tone 2
Lunar Tone of Challenge
Stabilize Energy - Stabilize!

At Tone 2 you start balancing or stabilizing the energy you received. Number 2 inherently contains polarity. Visualize 2 dots on an empty sheet of paper. Your eyes continuously move from one dot to the next. We can see this polarity in our Moon: she takes care of our soil hydrology, whereas not a drop of water can be found on her. She is our opposite. Tone 2 is the lunar Tone that you can use to take a close look at your opposite in the process: what are your obstacles and what is your challenge?

Features: *people with Tone 2 always see the other side of the coin, and they love to tell you about it. They may seem self-willed, but they mean to create balance. Unfortunately this often causes conflict. They are open and friendly and seem to know everybody. Behind that cover, however, hides a mystical side that only few people get to see.*

Tone 3
Electric Tone of Service
Bond Energy - Activate!

Visualize 3 dots in a space: a triangle. A pleasant activity arises: you have a choice! Standing on one of the dots, you can travel in 2 directions. There is movement and activity. That is why this is the Electric Tone. Where there are 2, a third one is needed in order to connect. This connecting energy can be used in the process of 13 in order to find a link between yourself, your purpose and a third factor: the external world, your boss, your client, the environment...How can you serve them with your activity?

Features: people with Tone 3 are artistic and expressive. They are often able to express themselves very well. They are excellent at bringing together people, targets and means. They can be very good mediators. They might possibly lose themselves in the process of mediation, forgetting who they are and what they want. Seclusion helps in such cases. They like being alone from time to time.

Tone 4
Self-Existing Tone of Form
Measure Energy - Define!

4 Is the number in which something is formed in the third dimension. Whereas 3 dots still form a plane, at least 4 dots are necessary to create a shape, something that can exist on its own. That's why we call Tone 4 the Self-Existing Tone. In this third dimension, time is our fourth dimension. We need time in order to experience the third dimension. Imagine a building; by moving through its space, you experience that space. You can estimate for instance the size of the walls. You 'measure' by moving your body. By measuring, you create or define the scope.

Features: people with Tone 4 are practical, realistic and well grounded. Sometimes their anchoring is so steady, they find it hard to change their mind once they have made it up, even when their fixed opinion no longer serves a purpose! It is wise to let go of that rigidity. People with Tone 4 are good at defining and determining limits. Furthermore they are skilled summarizors, translators and planners.

Tone 5
Overtone of Radiance
Command Energy - Confirm!

Tone 5 takes you back to the direction of the wind where you started in the cycle of 4: red-white-blue-yellow. That is why Tone 5 is called the OverTone. When this cycle is added to the previous one, a direct intensification of energy takes place. You can use this to strengthen yourself. Confirm! Show who you really are!

Features: people with Tone 5 are inquisitive, they want to know everything. Sometimes even too much, some would say...However, you want insight in the total picture. How does he do it? Where can you buy that? Why do you do it this way? This may cause your head to be swimming from time to time. Remember yourself. People with Tone 5 make their presence felt while in the company of others. They wish to be seen. After all, they have a lot to share...

Tones

Tone 6
Rhythmic Tone of Equality
Balance Energy - Flow!

When you visualize 6 dots on a sheet of paper or on a dice, a rhythm is born. Without probably even noticing it, you start forming groups: 1 2, 1 2, 1 2. Or 1 2 3, 1 2 3. That is the rhythm. Each rhythm has a certain time that is equal, that's why we experience it as a rhythm. Thus, 6 is the Tone of equality. Just do whatever the rhythm asks of you: rock in time and let it flow...

Features: *people with Tone 6 are full of ideas to improve or refine all that is. They want everything to be divided fairly, although they sometimes have their own ideas about fairness. It is wise to be more tolerant and less judgmental. How? Just let it flow: by movement, by new knowledge, by letting go!*

Tone 7
Resonant Tone of Attunement
Inspire Energy - Become one!

In the process of 13, 7 is right in the middle. It is the middle column of the Tzolkin Calendar. It is the center of your body, your spine. There are no polarities in the middle. It is not about left or right, nor about past or future. Number 7 is about the center, about being in the Here and Now. Tune in and become one! Be in Spirit and receive inspiration.

Features: *people with Tone 7 are very empathic, since they are good resonators. They seem to know what goes on in someone else. They find it hard to focus on themselves and on what they want. But once they do know, they are quite steadfast. They work hard and independent to reach their target, something that causes much admiration from other people. This, however, can cause loneliness from time to time.*

Tone 8
Galactic Tone of Integrity
Model Energy - Harmonize!

If (in the process of 13, the Wavespell) you resonate with the whole at Tone 7, you can harmonize your activity with the whole at Tone 8. You start modeling and harmonizing what you received as inspiration at 7. Tone 8 is a doubling of Tone 4, giving shape. Galactic means referring to Galaxis, the Milky Way. This refers to the Galactic Calendar with the natural cycles. Those who live in harmony with nature live in integrity.

Features: *people with Tone 8 are open to new experiences. They have integrated various philosophies of life, which sometimes makes them look slightly eccentric. Yet they remain honest. On the inside and the outside they are the same person. People with Tone 8 like structure and control. That is their harmony. If you take away their structure, they can get really confused...*

Tone 9
Solar Tone of Intention
Realize Energy - Mobilize!

At this 9th Tone, you are very close to realizing your purpose. You can feel it pulsating in yourself to materialize it on this planet. However, it is not time yet. Your intention is 100% and you radiate energy like the sun. You are extremely contented with what you are about to realize. The power this emanates is so strong, you would almost forget you still have to manifest your action during the 10th step of the wavespell.

Features: people with Tone 9 are good at persisting and finishing. They know how to use the available amount of energy - which is quite a lot - over longer periods of time, without exhausting themselves. They are efficient, knowing the difference between useful and useless. They have an eye for details. Sometimes, however, they are quite depressed, thinking everything is useless. Could this be caused by the idea that they had already accomplished it all?

Tone 10
Planetary Tone of Manifestation
Produce Energy - Manifest!

Finally the time has come. The moment has come to realize your purpose and to manifest it here on Earth. It is no longer something that just took shape in your mind, you can now actually touch it. It becomes reality on this planet. That's why we call it Planetary Tone, the Tone of Manifestation.

Features: people with Tone 10 change raw material and information into something visible and tangible. They are designers, writers, artists. Sometimes their creation drive is so strong, they want to do too many things, getting lost in all of that. If that's the case, they end up working hard, but manifesting nothing...

Tone 11
Spectral Tone of Liberation
Release Energy - Integrate!

It is now time to let go of what you have created and to put in into the world. Let it integrate with its environment. Spectral energy is focused outwardly. Imagine you have written a book. You now see it in a shop for the first time. It has been integrated into the world of books. What a liberation! Your work has been done...

Features: people with Tone 11 are so busy putting things into this world, they sometimes forget to let an idea mature a bit before actually manifesting it. Don't give it all away too soon. Don't forget to nourish yourself. Tone 11 people are very outwardly focused. They don't miss much. They like challenges, they love to overcome obstacles.

Tones

Tone 12
Crystal Tone of Cooperation
Universalize Energy - Understand!

After letting go of your product, it is time to get together and evaluate the process. How did it go? How can it be improved? What is its strongest feature? Understand! This means looking at the project with a helicopter view. Observe it from above, like an eagle in the sky. That way you can see the whole, thus enabling yourself to make this process universal. Let all insights come together; everything will become crystal-clear!

Features: *people with Tone 12 know how to cooperate with others. They are great at bringing together various points of view, thus creating one clear overview. They listen well, they are good at giving sound advice. They have the power to bring new life into things.*

Tone 13:
Cosmic Tone of Presence -
Magical Flight - Live!

Time to rest. You may now enjoy what you have created and recharge for your next project. You don't have to do anything, you just have to be. Live! You are now at the magical place of what has been and what will be. It is the peace and quiet after having been at the highest point of the wave. Listen to the splashing sound of the little bubbles on the water.

Features: *people with Tone 13 can see right through illusions. You cannot fool them, they know when something is not right. Sometimes they find it difficult to adapt to changes. They might seem to be dreamers with their heads in the clouds. But don't be fooled, they are simply a step ahead in time, or they look at the world beyond this one...*

Tone and key words

#	TONE	TONE NAME	MAYAN NAME	ACTION	POWER	FUNCTION
1	•	MAGNETIC	Hun	attract	unify	purpose
2	••	LUNAR	Ca	stabilize	polarize	challenge
3	•••	ELECTRIC	Ox	bond	activate	service
4	••••	SELF-EXISTING	Can	measure	define	form
5	—	OVERTONE	Ho	command	empower	radiance
6	—•	RHYTHMIC	Uac	balance	organize	equality
7	—••	RESONANT	Uc	inspire	channel	attunement
8	—•••	GALACTIC	Vaxac	model	harmonize	integrity
9	—••••	SOLAR	Bolon	realize	pulse	intention
10	═	PLANETARY	Lahun	produce	perfect	manifestation
11	═•	SPECTRAL	Hun Lahun	release	dissolve	liberation
12	═••	CRYSTAL	Ca Lahun	universalize	dedicate	cooperation
13	═•••	COSMIC	Ox Lahun	transcend	endure	presence

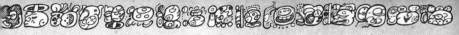

Solar Seal and key words

#	SOLAR SEAL	MAYAN NAME	ACTION	POWER	FUNCTION
1	DRAGON	Imix	nurture	birth	being
2	WIND	Ik	communicate	spirit	breath
3	NIGHT	Akbal	dream	abundance	intuition
4	SEED	Kan	target	flowering	awareness
5	SERPENT	Chicchan	survive	life force	instinct
6	WORLD-BRIDGER	Cimi	equalize	death	oppurtunity
7	HAND	Manik	know	accomplishment	healing
8	STAR	Lamat	beautify	elegance	art
9	MOON	Muluc	purify	universal water	flow
10	DOG	Oc	love	heart	loyalty
11	MONKEY	Chuen	play	magic	illusion
12	HUMAN	Eb	influence	free will	wisdom
13	SKYWALKER	Ben	explore	space	wakefulness
14	WIZARD	Ix	enchant	timelessness	receptivity
15	EAGLE	Men	create	vision	mind
16	WARRIOR	Cib	question	intelligence	fearlessness
17	EARTH	Caban	evolve	navigation	synchronicity
18	MIRROR	Etznab	reflect	endlessness	order
19	STORM	Cauac	catalyze	self-generation	energy
20/0	SUN	Ahau	enlighten	universal fire	life

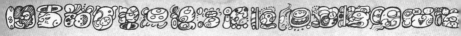

Solar Seals

There are 20 Solar Seals, suns or glyphs. Each one of them has its own quality and they all have the same value. The Seals follow a fixed sequence, which allows us to look at the 20 Seals as an evolution or a process. The first one is Dragon (number 1), arising from the deep oceans like the ancient dragon. Then comes Wind, bringing the breath of life necessary for all that lives. Then comes Night, bringing intuition and dreams. Everything is still perfect and abundant. Then there is Seed, with consciousness of the ego. That's when the Other is created. Serpent gives us the power of instinct, an original force aimed at survival, crawling up our spine like Kundalini energy. The Power of Death is called Worldbridger, teaches us that everything must end in order to be able to be reborn with full power. Hand brings satisfaction through creation. Star turns creation into great beauty, into art. Moon teaches us about our feelings, it shows us that they can change like the tides. Dog teaches us to be loyal, to love from the heart, even when our emotions tell us otherwise. Monkey reminds us not to be too serious and to dare to play again; life is beautiful! Human means freedom of choice. Choice is the result of wisdom, but it also carries the burden of responsibility. Skywalker gives us courage to choose a certain path… and to return if it turns out to be the wrong path. Wizard is aware of the power of all previous 13 Seals. That's why he closes his eyes and looks within, where all answers can be found. Eagle looks down on all answers and develops the vision to fly to whatever is closest to Father Sun. Warrior represents obtaining intelligence by asking questions, and Earth shows us the way by following our own feet to wherever they may lead us. Mirror reflects the endless order of the Cosmos, and Storm teaches us how to awaken this endless source of energy, so we can take our place in the cosmos as Sun, as an enlightened child of the source.

As you can see, all Seals are beautiful. None is more significant than the other. None can be excluded. We all have all of these qualities. The day you were born gives you a soul quality with which you follow your path on Earth. (See also 'your Galactic Signature')

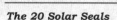

The 20 Solar Seals

We now present you with an overview of all the 20 Solar Seals, including the following features:

> **Image
> of the
> Solar Seal**

Mayan name: *in Yucateca, the language of the Mexican peninsula Yucatan.*

Pronunciation: *the phonetic pronunciation is put between brackets.*

Meaning: *which we included, since this calendar was also known to the Aztecs and other tribes.*

Direction of the wind: *every Seal goes with a certain color or direction of the wind, providing it with a certain energy.*

Key words: *every Seal has 3 key words: an action, a creative force and a function.*

Affirmation: *a brief poetic phrase easy to remember.*

Power: *a description of the original power of the Seal.*

Guidance: *focus to go through each day.*

Personality: *qualities of a person, linked to a Solar Seal.*

You can find the Wavespell description (i.e. the type of energy of a 13-day week) at the Moons.

__Affirmation__ (I am ...) by Rita van Vliet; __Power__ by Nicole E. Zonderhuis; __Guidance__ by Eden Sky; __Personality__ by Nicole E. Zonderhuis (based on Aluna's text, plus personal additions based on my own experience.)

1

2

Dragon - Imix (ee'mesh)

Dragon, crocodile.
Contains the initiating energy of the Red East.

Key words: *Nurtures, Birth, Being.*

Affirmation: *I am IMIX; DRAGON; I am your life source and womb. I support you, I feed you.*

Power: *Dragon is the ancient one rising from the deep ocean. In the beginning there was Dragon. He asked no questions, he knew exactly what he needed. He <u>was</u>. He trusted life unconditionally. Imix knows the beginning of time, it is from where we came and where we are going. Dragon is the power of the Primal Mother or the Inner Mother.*

Guidance: *Focus on self-nurturance and accepting the nurturance of the universe. Open your being to be intimately supported and provided for by life.*

Personality: *Dragon-people like to tell others about new discoveries and about their feelings. They are energetic, creative, nurturing and protecting, sometimes even in a parental way. They might forget to nurture themselves and to ask for what they really need. They are sensitive people and it would be good to be on their own. Imix is challenged to be freed of the feeling of rejection.*

Wind - Ik (eek')

Wind, air, breath, sometimes indicated as the letter T.
Contains the refining power of the White North.

Key Words: *Communicates, Breath, Spirit*

Affirmation: *I am IK; WIND; I am your Breath of Life and your Spirit. I inspire you to create your own truth and reality.*

Power: *Wind is like the Breath of Life necessary for all that lives. When God created man, he blew life into him with his own breath. Breathe in this Spirit, and inspiration will come your way. Breathe out and present your breath as a gift to Great Spirit/Hunab K'u. Your words will flow with this stream. Wind also means change: to trim one's sails according to the winds.*

Guidance: *Focus on Spirit's presence by acting on your natural inspiration. Let Spirit's breath guide you to communicate your truths.*

Personality: *Wind-people are very communicative and mental. They like talk and change. They are adroit, clever and have many faces. Wind is very idealistic and even romantic, he has trouble committing himself, making up his mind and taking responsibilities. He will find answers through education. Become the warm breeze gently touching the skin of those you love.*

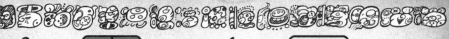

3

4

Night - Akbal (ok bol)

Night, house, temple, inner space. Contains the transformation power of the Blue West.

Key words: Dreams, Abundance, Intuition.

Affirmation: I am AKBAL, NIGHT; I am your place of mystery and unconsciousness. I give to you dreams and silence.

Power: The dark Night brings intuition and dreams. In the realm of dreams, there is only abundance. Everything is perfect. Night dares you to let go of your fear of shortage. Night represents the dark inner side of the temple of Self. Dare to go in and receive the gifts that are awaiting you. There is only abundance for those who have courage.

Guidance: Focus on entering the sanctuary of self - the inner darkness - the place of mystery within you. Unite with your stillness and intuition.

Personality: Night-people are strongly focused inwardly. They are thorough, thoughtful and self-reflective. Night feels a strong need to withdraw completely from time to time. He is a hard worker and does not easily give up. He finds it difficult to share and to inform. Night can be quite conservative; it is not easy for him to accept that other people have other opinions. Although he doesn't like to settle down in one particular place, it will do him good to create a safe haven, a place to return to where he feels emotionally secure and at home.

Seed - Kan (k'on)

Seed, corn, cat, lizard, iguana, frog. Contains the ripening power of the Yellow South.

Key words: Targets, Flowering, Awareness.

Affirmation: I am KAN; SEED; I am your creativity and sexuality. I give to you the power of growth and reproduction.

Power: The flower will be born from the seed, provided some conditions are met, such as fertile soil for nourishment, space and time to grow and sunlight to warm itself. The seed carries within itself all conditions necessary to grow. It is the seed of your creative and sexual power. Seed brings you the happiness of Self, like a baby who discovers his own hands, needing nothing else...

Guidance: Focus on the power of your intentions. Target your desires. Clarify. Plant the essential seeds. Expand and receive the natural growth of these desires.

Personality: Seed-people are enthusiastic, energetic and social, dedicated and naughty. They are natural leaders who like to be in the center of attention. Seed is a good networker, he recognizes the talents of others, but when will he start developing his own creative powers? He demands a lot from himself and he likes challenges. He cannot stand superficiality since he takes life quite seriously. Try to laugh and enjoy. Learn how to be patient. Seed has much ancient physical energy. Try to conduct this energy, don't let it turn into sexual obsessions or depressions. Outdoor activities, sports and artistic expressions can help.

5

6

Serpent - Chicchan (cheek chon)

Heavenly dragon, serpent.
Contains the initiating power of the Red East.

Key words: Survives, Life Force, Instinct

Affirmation: I am CHICCHAN, SERPENT; I am your life force and bodily wisdom. I give to you passion and desire.

Power: Serpent is the ancient energy that moves our body. Serpent energy or Kundalini spirals upwards, from the lowest chakra to the crown via the spine. Serpent awakens the treasures of the body through dance, movement and sensuality. Serpent teaches us to listen to our body and to enjoy it.

Guidance: Focus on the intrinsic wisdom of your body. Honor the perfection of your physical temple. Express your passion, vitality, and sensuality fully.

Personality: Serpent-people have a strong will, they are charismatic, spontaneous, passionate and bold. The Serpent is a good leader, a night person and he likes to be alone. He is the embodiment of instinct and the satisfaction of the senses. He is a person of extremes. He can be closed and withdrawn, yet he can also be extremely emotional. Serpent hates anger and rage; he tends to deny his own feelings and project them onto his environment. Movement and dance are excellent outlets for this intensity. They transform that raw energy.

Worldbridger - Cimi (kee me)

Death. Contains the refining power of the White North.

Key words: Equalizes, Death, Opportunity.

Affirmation: I am CIMI; Worldbridger; I am your ability to surrender and let go. I am your forgiveness and your liberation.

Power: Worldbridger is the power of death. He grants us understanding that death is merely a dividing line beyond which life continues. Death is part of life. If nothing dies, nothing can be born. Life is a cycle. Everything is life. Everything is a cycle. Death is but one of its faces. Worldbridger asks you to let go of your fear of death and loss. He asks you to forgive.

Guidance: Focus on allowing the necessary deaths to occur to create renewal and opportunities. Surrender your ego's need to control and relax into the Grace of the Larger Plan.

Personality: Worldbridger-people have a great sense of responsibility and duty. They are ambitious and good at cooperating and adapting to group spirit. Worldbridger takes his duties so seriously, that an intense longing for freedom arises. Money and beautiful things are important to him. In personal relationships, Worldbridger doesn't easily reveal himself. He tries to avoid this by wearing a mask. This behavior could be caused by fear of losing control. To surrender yourself is not the same as to give up! Keep the faith and relax.

7

8

Hand - Manik (ma neek')
Hand, deer, grip.
Contains the transformation power of the Blue West.

Key words: *Knows, Accomplishment, Healing.*

Affirmation: *I am MANIK; Hand; I am your artistic and healing abilities. I give to you beauty and accomplishment.*

Power: *Hand represents the power of 'having a grip'. Hand reaches out to the world to touch, integrate and understand everything. Those who have a grip, have understanding. Those who understand, have knowledge. Hand symbolizes everything we accomplish through our hands, including all material we transform into creation. It also means reaching out to other people. We carry the beauty of being human in our own hands.*

Guidance: *Focus on consciously evoking what you want to happen. Bring completion to the areas of your life that allow you to move to the next higher level of being. Enter the gateway of healing.*

Personality: *Hand-people are peaceful and generous, artistic, inspiring, hospitable and reliable. They love nature, animals and plants, but also good food and drinks. Being outdoors does them good. Hand is very fond of his personal freedom, he is quite individualistic, but - at the same time - loves good company and safety for his family. Being able to deal with these contradictory needs is his great challenge. He has difficulty finishing things, fearing he will not be contented with the result. It would do him good to focus more on the process instead of the end result.*

Star - Lamat (la mot)
Venus, rabbit.
Contains the ripening power of the Yellow South.

Key words: *Beautifies, Elegance, Art.*

Affirmation: *I am LAMAT; STAR; I show you the way. I give to you clarity and harmony.*

Power: *The power of Star is knowing when your creation is finished. Nothing more, nothing less. The power of Star is an inherent sense of harmony and the will to transform everything into beauty. Star is able to add just that little extra which gives his creation a surplus value, and only in a blink of an eye. Creation becomes art; it radiates beauty into the world.*

Guidance: *Focus on co-creating and extending harmony. Free the self-judgment and view your life as a work of art. As viewed so appears. Acknowledge beauty and art.*

Personality: *Star-people are energetic, busy, nervous, smart and playful. They love music, games, language and humor. They also love attention and are quite egocentric. Star is an intellectual and a complex person. Although harmony is his key word, Star just loves resistance and opposition. With his love for language and games, he is keen on purposefully taking an opposite position, rapping it up in sweet words, and then striking you down without mercy. At the same time, however, Star can be very insecure, worrying about other peoples' opinions. The answer can be found in redirecting his own energy and attention within, no matter how scary this might seem to be...*

9

10

Moon - Muluc (mul ok')

Water, rain, storm.
Contains the initiating power of the
Red East.

Key words: Purifies, Universal Water,
Flow.

Affirmation: I am MULUC; MOON;
I am your feeling and your consciousness. I help you remember GOD.

Power: The power of Moon is our
feeling. It is the world of emotions lying
at our feet and waiting to be entered.
Moon teaches us that emotions can
change like the tides. Just like water,
feelings need to flow in order to remain
healthy. Moon is all the water: the seas,
the rivers, the water in your body, the
water of the womb, your tears, your
sweat. Find it to purify yourself.

Guidance: Focus on purifying your
instrument of perception, your mind
and body, by intimately connecting
with your multi-dimensional self.
Nurture your body-world by anchoring
the vibration of your wholeness.
Energy flows where attention goes,
reunite with yourself by being awake
in the present moment.

Personality: Moon-people are very
emotional, romantic, variable, imagina-
tive and they can even be paranormally
gifted. Moon is a person of extremes. He
is both practical and emotional. He
needs limits and self-imposed control.
But even then he can be limitless. A safe
haven is a necessity. He is always prepared for the unexpected. This causes
others to be suspicious of him from time
to time. It makes him look like someone
with a hidden agenda. However, Moon
is totally sincere. Transforming his
hyper-sensitivity into sensitivity is his
great challenge. That is Moon's power.

Dog - Oc (ak)

Dog, feet.
Contains the refining power of the
White North.

Key words: Love, Heart, Loyalty.

Affirmation: I am OC; DOG; I am your
ability to love and to start again. I give
to you loyalty and help.

Power: The power of Dog can be
found in harmoniously living together
with someone else. Dog teaches us to
be loyal and to love from the heart,
even at times when our emotions tell
us to do otherwise. Dog shows us that
guiding and following are indeed
compatible in relationships. Dog
reminds you to be loyal to your own
ideals and your truth.

Guidance: Focus on transcending
limiting emotional patterns and
activating your spiritual strength in
relationship. Tune into the One Heart.
Unite with your companions of destiny.
Be loyal to your essence, your path,
and your kin.

Personality: Dog-people are very
loyal to friends and family. They are
cooperative, consistent, faithful and
helpful. Dog knows how to enjoy
himself. He is a good team player.
Approval and agreement of his
environment are important to him.
Growing up emotionally and dealing
with the role of his father/authority
are his great challenges. He sometimes
stubbornly refuses to see what's
really going on, due to his idealism. He
tends to measure by two standards in
relationships. One set of standards for
himself and another set for his partner.
Become aware of this, the intentions
are good...

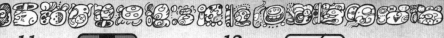

11

12

Monkey - Chuen (chew in)

Monkey.
Contains the transformation power of the Blue West.

Key words: *Plays, Magic, Illusion.*

Affirmation: *I am CHUEN; MONKEY; I am your spontaneity and magical child. I give to you humor and fun.*

Power: *The power of Monkey is the power of humor. Those who cannot laugh about themselves and their own actions, cause their own unhappiness. Let go of the illusion of your ego, be like a carefree child, rediscover your curiosity and open up to whatever life gives to you. Enjoy. Life is magically beautiful!*

Guidance: *Focus on celebrating your divine inner child through spontaneity and innocence. Laugh at yourself and disolve all seriousness. Lighten up! Enjoy the illusion. Apply humor and become invincible!*

Personality: *Monkey-people can be artistic, clever, inquisitive, playful and ostentatious. They need a lot of attention. With all that roleplaying, they might forget who they truly are. Others tend to forget that as well. What is real, what is illusion? Monkey is the playful and naughty child. With his humor and charm he twists everybody around his finger, as long as he doesn't put himself too much in the spotlight. He tends to deny his deep emotions and old pains by means of his humor, laughing away his own emotions. This may be an obstruction in intimate relationships. Having many creative outlets and an active social life are very important for Monkey.*

Human - Eb (eb)

Human, broom, tooth, dried grass.
Contains the ripening power of the Yellow South.

Key words: *Influences, Free Will, Wisdom.*

Affirmation: *I am EB; HUMAN; I am your free will... I give to you the wealth of going your own way.*

Power: *Human is the power of choice. Choice is an achievement of wisdom, but it also brings the burden of responsibility. Human is tough like dried grass and strong as a tooth; he is not easily defeated. He has the wisdom and the free will to influence his circumstances.*

Guidance: *Focus on choosing to be fueled with higher, expansive wisdom. Awaken the abilities of your human form by guiding your free-will with self-love. Enjoy your humanness. Honor your fellow human journeyers by extending wisdom.*

Personality: *Human-people are relaxed, well-mannered, cautious and helpful. From time to time, they can be sensitive, touchy and easily offended. Human is ambitious and a hard worker with an inquisitive mind. He will try many things, even when it doesn't serve him. But he is tough as grass and will get back on his feet again. Human has a tendency to suppress his anger. He often fears rejection. Making clear what it is he really wants is his great challenge. He needs to express his feelings and to cherish purifying and healing activities, in order to prevent his anger to destroy him.*

13

Skywalker - Ben (ben)

Reed, reed stem, corn stem, tube. Contains the initiating power of the Red East.

Key words: *Explores, Space, Wakefulness.*

Affirmation: *I am BEN; SKYWALKER; I am your messenger of the Light. I give to you the ability to travel through time and space.*

Power: *Too much choice can paralyze a man. The power of Skywalker gives you the courage to break new ground... and if necessary to turn around if your choice turns out to be a poor one. By opening up and being wakefull to what he finds on his chosen path, he knows whether or not it is the right path. Skywalker teaches us how to transform space, by using time as our ally.*

Guidance: *Focus on sharing sacred messages to unite Heaven and Earth. Face challenges and grow. Find empowerment in fluid reference points. Actively participate in creating the new future.*

Personality: *Skywalker-people are expressive, honest and prophetic. They could be the divine messenger. They have a broad interest. This makes them a bridge between different worlds, and great mediators. Skywalker is popular, talented, competent, he knows a lot and loves challenges. He is a crusader, fighting for principles and justice. Sometimes, his strict principles allow him to judge. It is important to be open to other points of view. That is where he can find the justice he strives for. He runs the risk to burn up when he is not well-balanced. He needs space, both physical and in a relationship.*

14

Wizard - Ix (eesh)

Wizard, magician, jaguar, ocelot. Contains the refining power of the White North

Key words: *Enchants, Timelessness, Receptivity.*

Affirmation: *I am IX; WIZARD; I am your knowledge from the heart... your shaman... I help you come to terms with the Divine Will.*

Power: *Wizard is aware of the power of all 13 previous seals. That is why he closes his eyes and looks within, where all answers can be found. Since Wizard enchants, he travels through the worlds without moving. He knows: once upon a time, there was no time. Receive the heart's wisdom, for you too can play magic!*

Guidance: *Focus on becoming the transparent wizard who allows magic to be effortlessly created through you. Use your heart-knowing to receive Divine Attunement. Be receptive to radial, non-linear, now-centered time.*

Personality: *Wizard-people can be paranormally gifted. They are good at putting abstractions into words or images. Wizard has a strong imagination. He is secretive, sensitive, proud and intelligent and he is interested in religion and spirituality. He is either a very good planner or a terrible one, not able to deal at all with the concept of time. Wizard understands the all-surrounding quality of time/space and of timelessness, but what is his own place? Wizard may tend to make feelings or situations look prettier than they actually are. What good does that do? Be loyal to yourself and let your heart speak.*

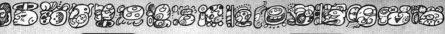

15

16

Eagle - Men (men)

Eagle, the wise one, cobweb, bird.
Contains the transformation power of
the Blue West.

Key words: Creates, Vision, Mind.

Affirmation: I am MEN; EAGLE; I am
your ability to build up relationships
and connections from a position of
independence. I give to you vision and
self-confidence.

Power: The power of Eagle is the
power of independent vision. Eagle
takes everything in at a glance and
develops the vision to fly to whatever
lies closest to Father Sun. Eagle
creates his own visions and dives right
into them.

Guidance: Focus on seeing the larger
plan, flying above like an eagle with
keen, clear sight. Use the power of
your mind to create, inspired by
commitment to your vision. Believe in
your connection to the Planetary Mind.

Personality: Eagle-people are independent, relaxed, intelligent and
ambitious. Sometimes they can be
shy. Eagle creates friendships in
which personal freedom is highly
respected. He bears in mind the well-
being of others. But he can also be
quite hard and critical on himself. He
might even be as demanding of others
as he is of himself, which will cause
other people to feel intimidated by him.
His independent nature drives him to
make great journeys or even to live like
a nomad. He finds it difficult to accept
that he cannot change the world on his
own...

Warrior - Cib (keeb)

Owl, vulture, turkey, crow.
Contains the ripening power of the
Yellow South.

Key words: Questions, Intelligence,
Fearlessness.

Affirmation: I am CIB; WARRIOR;
I am your inner knowledge and
wisdom. I take you to the other side
with gracious strength.

Power: The power of Warrior is obtaining intelligence by asking questions.
He is fearless and immovable. He does
not settle for half answers. He knows
how to continue getting answers.
Warrior is willing to fight for keeping or
extending the vision he just obtained.

Guidance: Focus on your inner voice
as you walk the path of the 'cosmic
question mark'. Advance towards your
fears. Be the warrior of grace.

Personality: Warrior-people are
serious, wise, realistic and pragmatic.
Their intuition is well developed. From
time to time they receive more information than they can handle. When that
happens, it's good to withdraw and
purify. Warrior may have a tough and
insensitive (even fatalistic) attitude,
due to old pain and disappointment.
Sometimes he makes life easier with
his sense of humor or by playing the
clown, quite often cynically and
sarcastically. He will not allow to be
dominated by others. Warrior needs to
learn that his personal power and
inner guidance doesn't have to be
threatened when others dominate him.

17

Earth - Caban (kah bon)

Earth, strength, incense, movement, earthquake. Contains the initiating power of the Red East.

Key words: Evolves, Navigation, Synchronicity.

Affirmation: I am CABAN; EARTH; I am your grounding and protection. I give to you earth power and crystal healing.

Power: The power of Earth is a warm guiding power. She leads the way, and you follow her like a magnet. It is almost like gravity, but Earth leads you in a horizontal direction. Follow your feet wherever they may lead. They walk the path of Mother Earth. Those who are good followers, will effortlessly walk in step with everything else. That is Synchronicity.

Guidance: Focus on synchronizing with your highest path. Navigate your time/space reality to open doors of evolution. Give and receive profound love to and from Mother Earth.

Personality: Earth-people are grounded, kind, mental, active, rationalizing, clever and practical. They are very convinced about their own ideas, holding on to them quite obstinately. Keep walking, Earth, that will do you good. Keep moving. Earth is a good leader and a terrible follower. His strong will often creates original solutions to problems. It'll do Earth good to be more flexible and patient, not to draw conclusions too soon, and to remain in the Here and Now.

18

Mirror - Etznab (ehts' nob)

Flint, knife, arrow head.
Contains the refining power of the White North.

Key words: Reflects, Endlessness, Order.

Affirmation: I am ETZNAB; MIRROR; I accept your shadow sides. I give to you purity and timelessness.

Power: Mirror is the power of perfection. It is the Tzolkin itself, containing a perfect order of numbers, which is a reflection of the order of the universe. It is a mirror behind a mirror, it is reality behind reality. It is Mirror that catches all the rays, subsequently reflecting it to the world as mirror image. What do you send out and what do you receive?

Guidance: Focus on discerning truth from illusion. Learn from the mirrors provided by other people and situations. Face your shadow and unconsciousness. Release all that does not authentically reflect you. Reflect the light of the Spiritual Warrior.

Personality: Mirror-people are practical and like to have a good view on things. They are social and empathic. To stay close to their own views and feelings is not easy for them, especially in intimate relationships. Mirror finds it easy to compromise, but doing so, he suppresses the anger he feels when those compromises do not reflect his wishes. Mirror feels the battle within between self-interest and sacrifice. The solution can be found in developing the ability to cooperate. Learn to use the sharp side of the mirror as a knife, whether to share with others or to cut the knot.

19

20/0

Storm - Cauac (kah wok)

Storm, rain of fire.
Contains the transformation power of the Blue West.

Key words: *Catalyzes, Self-Generation, Energy.*

Affirmation: *I am CAUAC; STORM; I bring disturbance in order to purify. I activate your light body and help you transform.*

Power: *Storm is a very strong power that can lift us off the ground and take us in its flow. It can shake us up and leave us behind. But inside a storm it is quiet. That is where we can find the eye of Storm, where we can learn how to generate the power of Storm in ourselves, so that we can always have access to this infinite source of energy.*

Guidance: *Focus on awakening the internal Thunderbeing! Catalyze transformation. Free up energy. Welcome the initiation of purification.*

Personality: *Storm-people are friendly and restless, with a youthful appearance. They have many faces, they are good students and good teachers. Storm has quite a lot of self-discipline and he is a perfectionist. He will fight for truth, which he will reveal ruthlessly. This will shake many people awake, often including himself. When it comes to intense emotions, Storm can be demanding and inflexible, trying to flee from reality in lust or addictions. Because of these extremes, Storm's greatest challenge is to remain human and approachable.*

Sun - Ahau (ah how)

Lord, hunter, flower, face.
Contains the ripening power of the Yellow South.

Key words: *Enlightens, Universal Fire, Life.*

Affirmation: *I am AHAU; SUN; I am your devotee and your Christ Consciousness. I give to you unconditional love and oneness.*

Power: *So there you are, full of energy and love, in the center of your life. The smile on your face comes from deep within. You are filled with peace. You are ready to take your place in this cosmos, just like the Sun, like an enlightened child of the Source.*

Guidance: *Focus on letting the radiance of your inner sun illuminate and empower your moments. Ascend into your heart center and access unconditional love. Bask in the power of your realized wholeness and freedom.*

Personality: *Sun-people are loving, dedicated, artistic, dreamy and romantic. They might seem to be dreamers with their heads in the clouds. They can be socially awkward, but they want the best for everybody. Due to their idealistic character, they can be stubborn and without compromise. It is Sun's great challenge to learn how to deal with disappointments caused by unrealistic expectations. It will do him good to keep life simple. Be like the Sun and radiate your love unconditionally into this world. Let your light shine on everyone and everything, including yourself!*

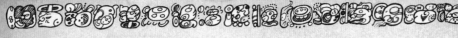

Hunab K'u

Hunab K'u is the heart of the Milky Way, the place the ancient Maya called the Cosmic Womb. Hunab K'u is the One Creator of Measure and Movement, the heart of the Milky Way where - according to the Maya - all measure and movement originates.

Hunab K'u radiates energy and information. It uses stars as lenses to send energy to the planets. To our Earth, the sun ('Kin' in Yucatec language) is the main transformer of Hunab K'u's energy. It is the lens through which the Earth receives direct galactic information. Hunab K'u's pulses are like a language or code/energy, encoded within the Tzolkin, a universal harmonic module containing every possible combination of Hunab K'u. It is the Sacred Calendar. Hunab K'u is the numerical connection between the numbers 13 and 20. They represent movement and measure, energy and shape, spirit and soul. Hunab K'u is geometrically represented by a square inside a circle.

Hunab K'u is the one and the other, but it is also neither the one, nor the other. It is masculine and feminine and yet it is neutral. In Guatemala they refer to it as: Heart of the Sky and Heart of the Earth. They give it the colors green and white, or green and pale blue.

"Hunab K'u radiates in everything,
the universe, the galaxies, the sun and the earth,
light and darkness and all that exists are mere songs of Hunab K'u.
Hunab K'u sleeps in all named and unnamed things."

It is up to you now to awaken Hunab K'u in your presence.

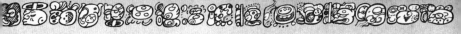

You now have several lists with data. All you have to do next is make combinations. Look at the color of the day, and you know what power that day has. Is it good for starting something (red) or for transforming something (blue)? As an example of the interpretation of the core words, I will explain the year energy. It is hard to fully understand the combination of Tone and Seal. After all, there are 260 different combinations. The words are the threads by which the image of the energy forms. You may just suddenly recognize the features of the energy in a day, a year or a person. Don't try too hard, it will come to you. All you have to do is remember...

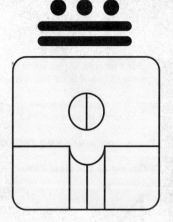

13 Seed year
Yellow Cosmic Seed Year
Mayan name: Ox Lahun Kan

	Action	Power	Function
13	Transcend	Endure	Presence
Seed	Targets/Ripen	Flowering	Awareness

Combining these keys, one gets:

> *endure flowering*
> *by transcending and ripening*
> *creating awareness and presence*

When something flowers, we normally refer to a temporary state of being. Enduring flowering sounds rather magical. It is a permanent state of growth, being open to the entire cosmos in all its beauty, like a wide open flower spreading its colors and its scent.

Being aware of a presence refers to an unusual state of brightness, in which you are fully aware of the presence of the Great Spirit in everything that surrounds us.

The way to achieve this, is by transcending and ripening. By transcending and taking to a higher level that which is not yet whole. And by letting the seeds ripen that have been sown in the past. It requires faith to wait and let nature do its work. Create a warm spot in the sun and a good, fertile soil. (Manure if necessary).

In the journal you find the description of 1 Moon Year.

Calculate your Galactic Signature

*The day you were born on the 13-Moon Calendar
is your Galactic Signature.*

*Your Galactic Signature is one of the 260 different possibilities shown on the
Galactic Calendar / Tzolkin (page 42).*

To find your Galactic Signature, follow the steps below.

*Step 1. What Gregorian year were you born?
  Find the Year # for your birth year in the chart to the right.*

*Step 2. Take the Year Number you found in Step One and add the number
  you find next to the Gregorian month you were born (chart right).*

*Step 3. Now add the number of the day you were born in that month.
  For example, if you were born on November 28, add 28 (February 29 is not
  counted on the 13-Moon calendar, just count it as February 28 and continue.)*

*Step 4. If the total number you have added is greater than 260,
  you need to subtract 260.*

Step 5. Look over on the Tzolkin on page 42 and find your Galactic Signature.

Welcome to the New Time!

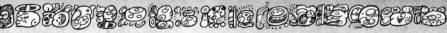

(Step 1)

Gregorian year of birth			Year #
2013	1961	1909	217
2012	1960	1908	112
2011	1959	1907	7
2010	1958	1906	162
2009	1957	1905	57
2008	1956	1904	212
2007	1955	1903	107
2006	1954	1902	2
2005	1953	1901	157
2004	1952	1900	52
2003	1951	1899	207
2002	1950	1898	102
2001	1949	1897	257
2000	1948	1896	152
1999	1947	1895	47
1998	1946	1894	202
1997	1945	1893	97
1996	1944	1892	252
1995	1943	1891	147
1994	1942	1890	42
1993	1941	1889	197
1992	1940	1888	92
1991	1939	1887	247
1990	1938	1886	142
1989	1937	1885	37
1988	1936	1884	192
1987	1935	1883	87
1986	1934	1882	242
1985	1933	1881	137
1984	1932	1880	32
1983	1931	1879	187
1982	1930	1878	82
1981	1929	1877	237
1980	1928	1876	132
1979	1927	1875	27
1978	1926	1874	182
1977	1925	1873	77
1976	1924	1872	232
1975	1923	1871	127
1974	1922	1870	22
1973	1921	1869	177
1972	1920	1868	72
1971	1919	1867	227
1970	1918	1866	122
1969	1917	1865	17
1968	1916	1864	172
1967	1915	1863	67
1966	1914	1862	222
1965	1913	1861	117
1964	1912	1860	12
1963	1911	1859	167
1962	1910	1858	62

(Step 2)

Gregorian month of birth	
January	0
February	31
March	59
April	90
May	120
June	151
July	181
August	212
September	243
October	13
November	44
December	74

Examples:

October 9, 1940 John Lennon

1940:	92
Oct.:	13
day:	9

total = 114 = 10 Wizard

December 30, 2005 start of
new Tzolkin-cycle

2005:	157
Dec.:	74
day:	30

total = 261 - 260 = 1 = 1 Dragon

Galactic Signature: your personal 'kin'

The Tone-Seal combination of the day you were born, determines your personal 'kin'. We call this your 'Galactic Signature'. You are a Galactic being, for you are part of the entire Creation. You decided to start your path here on Earth the day you were born. That particular moment gives you a special energy and destination. You could call it your Mayan horoscope, which contains a lot of information. Your Color is the source of your power, your Tone is the function of creative contribution and your Solar Seal is your archetypical essence of power.

Each Solar Seal is guided on its path of life by four other kin (see table alongside):
- *a guide kin* (= a guiding power) walks in front of you (above in the table)
- *an analog kin* (= helping power) walks on your right side
- *an occult kin* (= hidden power) walks behind you (below in the table)
- *an antipode kin* (= challenge power) walks on your left side

Except for the guide, the other 3 kin are fixed for each Seal. For example, each Skywalker has a Night as its Antipode. You can find them in the table on the next page. The main Seal is always in de middle. Notice that if someone is your analog (or occult or antipode), you are also his / her analog (or occult or antipode).

What does this mean?

We call this your Destiny Oracle: it is the Galactic Signature surrounded by the four Seals accompanying you. But what does it mean? People or days with this Solar Seal can be of help on your path of life. Think of them as good friends.
A Guide gives you good advice and shows you the way.
The Analog is your soulmate, you understand each other without words.
The Antipode is the one that challenges you, he tells you the truth even if you don't want to hear it. The Occult could be someone you don't consider to be one of your friends, but he/she does help you. Aluna Joy Yaxk'in sees the Occult as a shadow: the shadow refers to everything that has been repressed. It embodies everything in life that is denied expression. It is like a mirror.

Find your Guide.

Your guide is always one of the Seals of your color. Which Seal it is, depends on the Tone.
1) What is the Tone of your 'Galactic Signature'?
2) Check your next step
        Tone 1, 6 and 11 guide themselves
        Tone 2, 7 and 12 go back 8 Seals
        Tone 3, 8 and 13 proceed 4 Seals
        Tone 4 and 9 go back 4 Seals
        Tone 5 and 10 proceed 8 Seals
3) Find your Seal in the row below and count forwards or backwards
   (or stay where you are).

4) The Seal you end up with is your guide.
   For example: my Tone is 10, so I go forward 8 Seals starting at my Seal:
   the Skywalker. I end up with Dragon. Thus Dragon is my Guide.

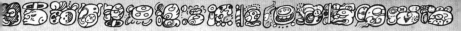

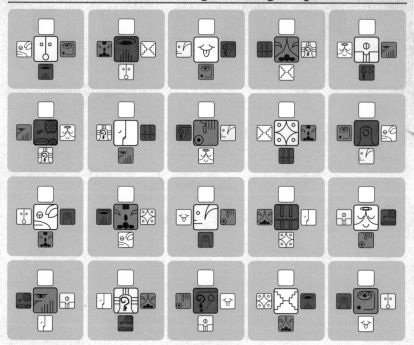

Tones

The Tones are equal to your Tone, except the one of your occult power.
Your occult power added up to your Tone equals 14.
For example: my Tone is 10, so the Tone of my occult power is 4: I am
10 Skywalker, so my occult is 4 Star.

Now what?

If you know how it works, you can add your Signature to your personal data
in your diary. You can also make a list of the Seals and Tones of your family
members and friends in the 'who-is-who' table. Maybe one of them is the perfect
guide for you. (Perfect meaning similar Tones as well.) You can also add it to
your address book.

Have Fun!

In Lak'ech

- Yucatec Mayan Code of Honor:
'I am Another Yourself'

Who is who?

(Fill in the names of your family, friends and relatives.)

seal → / tone ↓					
•					
••					
•••					
••••					
—					
—•					
—••					
—•••					
—••••		Lloydine Arguëlles			
═					
═•					
═••					
═•••					

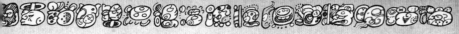

Who is who?

▯	▣	◇	◗	⊞	← seal ↓ tone
					•
					••
					•••
					••••
					—
					—•
					—••
					—•••
					—••••
					═
					═•
			Herman J. Hegge		═••
					═•••

75

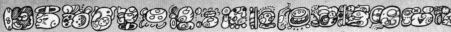

Who is who?

(Fill in the names of your family, friends and relatives.)

seal → / tone ↓					
•					
••					
•••					
••••			Eden Sky		
—					
—•					
—••					
—•••					
—••••					
=			Nicole E. Zonderhuis		
=•	José Argüelles				
=••		Sylvia Carrilho			
=•••					

76

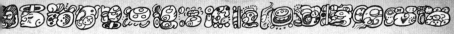

Who is who?

					← seal ↓ tone
					•
					••
					•••
					••••
					▬
					•̲
					••̲
					•••̲
					••••̲
					▬▬
					•̲̲
					••̲̲
					•••̲̲

77

How to use

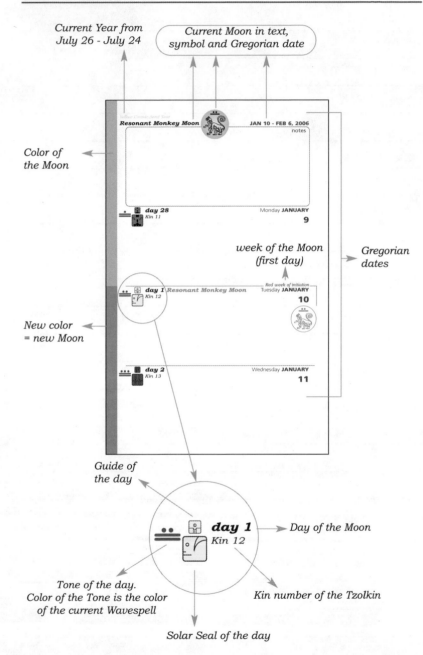

Current Year from July 26 - July 24

Current Moon in text, symbol and Gregorian date

Resonant Monkey Moon

JAN 10 - FEB 6, 2006
notes

Color of the Moon

day 28
Kin 11

Monday **JANUARY**
9

week of the Moon (first day)

Red week of initiation
day 1 *Resonant Monkey Moon*   Tuesday **JANUARY**
Kin 12   **10**

Gregorian dates

New color = new Moon

day 2
Kin 13

Wednesday **JANUARY**
11

Guide of the day

day 1   → Day of the Moon
Kin 12

Tone of the day.
Color of the Tone is the color of the current Wavespell

Kin number of the Tzolkin

Solar Seal of the day

This is the first day of the
260-day cycle. That's why you
find Kin number 1 next to the
pictograph of December 30.
A good place to start the diary!
This year, it's very close to
January 1. How convenient!

> This is a GAP,
> one of the 52 dark
> (or black) sections in the
> Galactic Calendar.

> Bigger Seal
> indicates the start
> of a Wavespell.

DECEMBER Friday

30

day 18
Kin 1
GAP

DECEMBER Saterday

31

day 19
Kin 2

JANUARY Sunday

1
New Year's Day

day 20
Kin 3

Here you can find quotes related to the day seal. For example, next week it is a 'Dog-day'
with the keywords: love, heart and loyalty. See how the quote makes sense.

notes

---

day 21
Kin 4

Monday **JANUARY**

2

day 22
Kin 5

Tuesday **JANUARY**

3

---

day 23
Kin 6

Wednesday **JANUARY**

4

Yellow Cosmic Seed Year

Rhythmic Lizard Moon

JANUARY Thursday

5

day 24

Kin 7

JANUARY Friday

6

day 25

Kin 8

JANUARY Saterday

7

day 26

Kin 9

JANUARY Sunday

8

day 27

Kin 10

"Our heart can be strong where it has been broken."
- Jack Kornfield -

January 10 - February 6
Totem animal: Monkey
Dominant Tone: Tone 7 - inspire, channel, attunement

Monkey

The Maya made a distinction between the monkeys of the animal kingdom and supernatural God Monkeys, such as Hun Chuen, who granted man the ability to write. The monkeys of the animal kingdom remind the Maya of a period in time they might prefer to forget... The following describes the story of creation from the Pop Wuj, the Sacred Scripture of the Maya.

After Earth had been created with all her plants and animals, the Gods wanted to create beings that would call upon them and worship them. From the soil they created Man. But the soil was soft and it fell apart when it got wet. Creator and Designer then carefully carved sculptures from wood. They seemed like real people and they populated Earth. They got sons and daughters, yet they had no soul and no mind. They walked endlessly on their hands and feet. They were responsible for the animal pets, but treated them badly. They showed no respect towards their environment and destroyed Earth shamelessly. One day, all the animals - large and small - and all the furnishings - pots and pans - revolted against the Wooden Man. And the Gods themselves were discontented. The Wooden Man did not remember its creators, Heart of the Sky and Heart of the Earth. Thus, Heart of the Sky caused a flood, washing away every Wooden Man. The Wooden Man ran for his life. He tried to climb on the roof of his house, but all the houses collapsed. They sought shelter in trees, but the trees shook them off. They fled into caves, but the caves closed themselves. A few Wooden Men managed to flee into the mountains where they still live today as monkeys...

The sacred clown

Even today many people dress up as monkeys during Mayan feasts. Monkeys still have a special function. They make jokes - some of which are quite rude - and tell people what they can and cannot do. They function like the Heyokas of the Native Americans, the sacred clowns. They too teach people about norms and values, by setting a poor example themselves.

Channel

The Monkey reminds us to attune to the world around us, to be a channel for that. Number 7 is right in the middle between Tone 1 and 13. Tone 7 represents the spine, the only joint in the center of your body. It is a channel. Be in your center and become a channel. Let energy flow right through you, from top to bottom and back up again. Inspiration will then follow.

Inspiration

This is a Moon to get inspired! The Monkey is a cheerful clown, always ready for a joke. It is the inner child, still without negative experiences, who lets everything flow freely. Let it flow and be inspired! That can lead to wonderful creative processes such as painting and writing. The ancient Maya believed it was the Monkey who gave mankind the ability to write. Ancient images show the Monkey over a book or codex bound in jaguar skin, holding a pen in his hand.

Dragon Wavespell

Man has a tendency to control, change or improve his environment. This Wavespell is about letting things be the way they are. Do not complain when it rains, but cherish the wet drops falling on your head. Do not get upset in traffic. It is the way it is. Be like a tree that watches the world around it, free of judgement and without wanting to change anything. Cherish life just the way it is. Be your own mother and give yourself what it is you truly need. Cherish your belly and your womb as the source of all life.

Wizard Wavespell

Maybe you already found out in the Dragon Wavespell just how difficult it is to let love really in. This Wavespell is there to sit back and see whatever good presents itself. Feel how difficult it is not to take any action. When something presents itself, dare to let it in. If any questions arise these days, consult your heart where all the answers can be found. Past and future come together in your heart. Try to keep both feet on the ground in order not to be taken over by timelessness; you might 'lose' a few moments...

Hand Wavespell

'Knowing' is one of the key words of Hand. Hand 'knows' because he is curious and he cannot stand not being in control. Hand wants to 'grab understanding'. This Wavespell you will be challenged in this area. Maybe there is more than you can or need to understand. Or maybe the right knowledge or teacher will reveal itself/himself. It is now time to literally focus on your hands. Look well after them and let them do what they like to do. Do they want to model clay, do they want to draw, write or massage? Especially creative processes that are manifested through your hands, are healing. Don't give up too easily, this is about accomplishment. To let something be untouched, will not make you happy. It will, however, if you pick it up and deal with it.

notes

day 28
Kin 11

Monday **JANUARY**

9

Red week of initiation

day 1 *Resonant Monkey Moon*
Kin 12

Tuesday **JANUARY**

10

day 2
Kin 13

Wednesday **JANUARY**

11

JANUARY Thursday

12

day 3

Kin 14

        o

JANUARY Friday

13

day 4

Kin 15   o o

JANUARY Saterday

14

day 5

Kin 16   o o o

JANUARY Sunday

15

day 6

Kin 17   o o o o

"Your dreams and wishes will show you the way"
- anonymous -

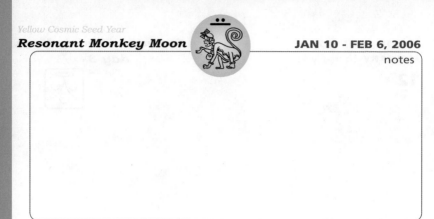

notes

day 7
Kin 18

Monday **JANUARY**

16

day 8
Kin 19

White week of refinement
Tuesday **JANUARY**

17

day 9
Kin 20
GAP

Wednesday **JANUARY**

18

JAN 10 - FEB 6, 2006

Yellow Cosmic Seed Year

Resonant Monkey Moon

JANUARY Thursday
19

day 10
Kin 21

JANUARY Friday
20

day 11
Kin 22
GAP

JANUARY Saterday
21

day 12
Kin 23

JANUARY Sunday
22

day 13
Kin 24

---

*"Use what talent you possess - the woods would be very silent if no birds sang except
those that sang best."*
- Henry Van Dyke (1852) -

notes

day 14
Kin 25

Monday **JANUARY**

23

_____ *Blue week of transformation*
day 15
Kin 26

Tuesday **JANUARY**

24

day 16
Kin 27

Wednesday **JANUARY**

25

JANUARY Thursday
26

day 17
Kin 28 ••

JANUARY Friday
27

day 18
Kin 29 •••

JANUARY Saterday
28

day 19
Kin 30 ••••

JANUARY Sunday
29

day 20
Kin 31

*"Never ever doubt in magic. The purest honest thoughts come from children,
ask any child if they believe in magic and they will tell you the truth."
- Scott Dixon - 10 Eagle*

Yellow Cosmic Seed Year

Resonant Monkey Moon

JAN 10 - FEB 6, 2006

notes

---

day 21
Kin 32

Monday **JANUARY**

30

Yellow week of ripening

 **day 22**
Kin 33

Tuesday **JANUARY**

31

---

day 23
Kin 34

Wednesday **FEBRUARY**

1

FEBRUARY Thursday

2

day 24

Kin 35

FEBRUARY Friday

3

day 25

Kin 36

FEBRUARY Saterday

4

day 26

Kin 37

FEBRUARY Sunday

5

day 27

Kin 38

---

*"Order is a lovely nymph, the child of Beauty and Wisdom; her attendants are Comfort,
Neatness, and Activity; her abode is the valley of happiness: she is always to be found when
sought for, and never appears so lovely as when contrasted with her opponent, Disorder."
- Samuel Johnson - 5 Mirror*

Galactic Hawk Moon

February 7 - March 6
Totem animal: Hawk
Dominant Tone: Tone 8 - model, harmonize, integrity

Galactic Moon

Galactic means: referring to Galaxis, the Milky Way. The Maya looked upon life on Earth as being connected with our solar system and all of the cosmos. Whereas we think the sun rises in the east and sets in the west via the south, the Maya already knew that the Earth itself orbits left (counter clockwise) and that this is why the sun seems to be moving from left to right. It is as if they looked down on the entire Milky Way from above. That's how their calendar was set up. They knew what we have only recently discovered: the Earth not only orbits around its own axis (24 hours) and around the sun (1 year), but we also orbit - together with the sun - in 26,000 years around the central sun of the Pleiades: Alcyone. To them, our relationship with the Milky Way is part of our every day reality. The 260-day Tzolkin is a fractal of this cycle.

Do I live what I believe in?

During the previous Moon you attuned yourself to the Great Spirit and to your surroundings. During this Moon it is time to truly attune your actions to just that, to be in harmony with the Great Spirit, in word and deed. Integrity is when form and contents are in harmony, when you are truly honest. In order to achieve this, you will have to look down onto your life, like a hawk on the wing.

The first day of the Moon = 1 Sun

The first day of the Moon is a day with Solar Seal Sun. This month you will be confronted with the question just how honest you are when it comes to giving and receiving unconditional love. Do you get enough unconditional love and can you receive it? Do you fear that the other one expects something in return? How unconditional are you really?

Model
In the cycle of 4 (red, white, blue, yellow), 8 is the intensification of the action of Tone 4. 'To model' is the intensification of 'measuring and defining'. That which you still only observed at Tone 4, is now materialized.

Hawk
The Hawk is the 'Messenger'. The Hawk flies close to the light of Grandfather Sun and brings us the message of the light. The Hawk's shrieking cry enters your subconsciousness and asks you to search for the truth. During the Hawk Moon, you may receive messages from the realm of our Grandfathers and Grandmothers. Open up to these messages and recognize them when you receive them. The power of the Hawk is close to the Skywalker, it is the prophetic messenger. The Hawk flies close to the light of Grandfather Sun. This requires a sharp eye and a bold heart. The Hawk's attentiveness is impressive, he can see from a great distance and looks down on past and future. Be attentive and learn to look at your environment. Observe the ordinary in everything you do. Life gives signs. Life itself is the initiation.

Sun Wavespell
The Sun represents the universal fire that enlightens and warms all life. Be like the Sun and radiate your love unconditionally into this world. Ask yourself the question how unconditional your deeds really are. What are the hidden motives or expectations? If these are not entirely pure, you might be disappointed this Wavespell. This Solar Seal is also known as a Flower or a Face. Notice how this is presented these days.

Skywalker Wavespell
The Skywalker Wavespell asks you to pay attention. You might be confronted with choices or you might start doubting whether or not you have taken the right path. By being open and perceptive to whatever you come across on your path, you will know whether you have taken the right path or not. Skywalker is also about courage: the courage to turn around when you realize you took the wrong path, the courage to speak your truth, the courage to leave the safe nest and to discover the world. Keep moving, that is Skywalker's assignment, both in situations and in ideas.
"Those who remain with both feet on the ground, don't get very far", Loesje.

Worldbridger Wavespell
During this Wavespell we continue to let go and forgive: the power of Worldbridger. Before we can enter new paths, we sometimes have to get rid of some lumber. Ask yourself the question whether or not possessions, situations, judgements or ideas still serve you, or whether they keep you from moving on. The Wavespell challenges you, so you can be sure you will encounter everything you need to let go of or forgive. Any resistance is the result of your fear of death. Realize you don't fully live if you can't look at death as a consequence of life.

notes

 day 28
Kin 39
GAP

Monday **FEBRUARY**

6

Red week of initiation

day 1 *Galactic Hawk Moon*
Kin 40

Tuesday **FEBRUARY**

7

day 2
Kin 41

Wednesday **FEBRUARY**

8

FEBRUARY Thursday

9

day 3
Kin 42

- - -

FEBRUARY Friday

10

day 4
Kin 43
GAP

- - - -

FEBRUARY Saterday

11

day 5
Kin 44

FEBRUARY Sunday

12

day 6
Kin 45

-

---

*"Our own physical body possesses a wisdom which we who inhabit the body lack.
We give it orders which make no sense."*
- Henry Miller - 13 Hand

notes

---

day 7
Kin 46

Monday **FEBRUARY**

13

White week of refinement
Tuesday **FEBRUARY**

day 8
Kin 47

14

---

day 9
Kin 48

Wednesday **FEBRUARY**

15

Yellow Cosmic Seed Year
Galactic Hawk Moon

FEBRUARY Thursday

16

day 10
Kin 49

FEBRUARY Friday

17

day 11
Kin 50
GAP

FEBRUARY Saterday

18

day 12
Kin 51
GAP

FEBRUARY Sunday

19

day 13
Kin 52

"We can influence who we will be tomorrow, for tomorrow can only be built on today."
- Anne Wilson Schaef -

notes

---

day 14
Kin 53

Monday **FEBRUARY**

20

Blue week of transformation
day 15
Kin 54

Tuesday **FEBRUARY**

21

---

day 16
Kin 55

Wednesday **FEBRUARY**

22

FEBRUARY Thursday

23

day 17 • • • •

Kin 56

FEBRUARY Friday

24

day 18

Kin 57

FEBRUARY Saterday

25

day 19 •

Kin 58

GAP

FEBRUARY Sunday

26

day 20 • •

Kin 59

"No one would have crossed the ocean if he could have gotten off the ship in the storm."
- Charles Kettering - 9 Skywalker

day 21
Kin 60

Monday **FEBRUARY**

27

Yellow week of ripening

day 22
Kin 61

Tuesday **FEBRUARY**

28

day 23
Kin 62

Wednesday **MARCH**

1

MARCH Thursday

2

day 24

Kin 63

MARCH Friday

3

day 25

Kin 64

GAP

MARCH Saterday

4

day 26

Kin 65

MARCH Sunday

5

day 27

Kin 66

○

"People fear death even more than pain. It's strange that they fear death. Life hurts a lot more than death. At the point of death, the pain is over. Yeah, I guess it is a friend."
- Jim Morrison - 8 Moon

March 7 - April 3
Totem animal: Jaguar
Dominant Tone: Tone 9 - realize, pulse, intention

Jaguar

To the Maya, the Jaguar was a symbol of great strength. He was associated with the power of the elite. This animal was so sacred, only high-priests were allowed to wear robes of jaguar skin. In the spots of the jaguar fur they saw an image of the starry sky. And we know by now that whoever understands the cycles of the stars, understands the cycles of the Earth. Even sacrificial altars were made in the shape of a jaguar, just like the thrones on which the rulers were portrayed.

The Maya called the jaguar Balaam or Chac (the Rain God). Balaam also means mysterious or occult. The word Chilam means a group of priests who explain the oracle and who predicted the future. The books of the Chilam Balaam are the Sacred Scriptures of the Mayan priests.

The Jaguar equals Solar Seal Wizard. For a shaman it is the greatest test and achievement to transform into a jaguar. The Jaguar God of the underworld often appeared as an owl. Maybe that's why the glyph for Wizard so starkly resembles an owl.

Solar Moon

During the 9th Moon, the realization of your purpose is getting very close. You can feel the energy pulsating in yourself to bring it into existence here on Earth. However, it is not time yet. After the harmonization with Galaxis we once again return to the Sun in order to get some more energy. That's why this Moon is called the Solar Moon, named after Sol (Sun). You want to charge your intention with solar energy. You are as good as full of that which you are about to realize. The power this emanates is so strong, you would almost forget you still have to manifest your action during the 10th Moon. Before swinging into action, it is wise to once more become the Jaguar who stalks his prey. Consider your options and the details of your plan before you attack. Let the tension of the action pulsate across your fur to the tip of your tail.

The first day of the Moon: 3 Star

When you ask yourself the question: "How do I reach my target?", you can include the energy of the first day of this Moon - the Yellow Electric Star - in your consideration. This is the energy of the Activation of Beauty.

Worldbridger Wavespell

During this Wavespell we continue to let go and forgive: the power of Worldbridger. Before we can enter new paths, we sometimes have to get rid of some lumber. Ask yourself the question whether or not possessions, situations, judgements or ideas still serve you, or whether they keep you from moving on. The Wavespell challenges you, so you can be sure you will encounter everything you need to let go of or forgive. Any resistance is the result of your fear of death. Realize you don't fully live if you can't look at death as a consequence of life.

Storm Wavespell

If - after the previous two Wavespells - there are still things you don't really want to face, the Storm Wavespell will be merciless. It will not be subtle, after all, a soft storm is no storm. Know, however, that this only occurs to purify and transform you. If everything remains calm in your life, don't forget you might end up in somebody else's storm. Remain calm. Storm also gives you great power; you have much energy to deal with all sorts of things. Put your shoulder to the tread wheel!

Human Wavespell

Man has Free Will, but do you really want to choose? In the western world, freedom of choice has become a burden. What do I want to eat? What newspaper do I want to read? Whom do I want to see? Where do I want to go? There is so much choice, we often end up in 'who, what, where, which' too soon, skipping the first question: "Do I want to...?" Ask yourself what it is you really want.
The Solar Seal Human also represents teeth: take well care of your teeth. Pay attention these 13 days to whether or not (and if so, how?) others are trying to influence you. Also pay attention to whether or not you yourself are trying to influence others.

notes

○ ○ **day 28**
Kin 67

Monday **MARCH**

6

○ ○ ○ **day 1** *Solar Jaguar Moon*
Kin 68

Red week of initiation
Tuesday **MARCH**

7

○ ○ ○ ○ **day 2**
Kin 69
GAP

Wednesday **MARCH**

8

MARCH Thursday

9

day 3
Kin 70

MARCH Friday

10

day 4
Kin 71
○

MARCH Saterday

11

day 5
Kin 72
○ ○
GAP

MARCH Sunday

12

day 6
Kin 73
○ ○ ○

"It's better to explore life and make mistakes than to play it safe.
Mistakes are part of the dues one pays for a full life."
- Sophia Loren - 11 Serpent

notes

○○○○
day 7
Kin 74

Monday **MARCH**
13

White week of refinement
Tuesday **MARCH**
14

day 8
Kin 75

day 9
Kin 76

Wednesday **MARCH**
15

MARCH Thursday

16

day 10

Kin 77

GAP

MARCH Friday

17

day 11

Kin 78

MARCH Saterday

18

day 12

Kin 79

MARCH Sunday

19

day 13

Kin 80

---

*"You can never understand the tremendous peace that is always there within you,
that is your natural state. Your trying to create a peaceful state of mind is in fact
creating a disturbance within you."*
- U.G. Krishnamurti -

notes

---

day 14
Kin 81

Monday **MARCH**

Spring equinox **20**
126 PM EST
- 1826 GMT

Blue week of transformation

day 15
Kin 82

Tuesday **MARCH**

21

---

day 16
Kin 83

Wednesday **MARCH**

22

Yellow Cosmic Seed Year
Solar Jaguar Moon

MARCH Thursday

23

day 17
Kin 84

MARCH Friday

24

day 18
Kin 85
GAP

MARCH Saterday

25

day 19
Kin 86

MARCH Sunday

26

day 20
Kin 87

"Our greatest glory is not in never falling, but in rising every time we fall."
- Confucius -

notes

 ***day 21***
Kin 88
GAP

Monday **MARCH**
27

Yellow week of ripening
Tuesday **MARCH**
28

 day 22
Kin 89

 day 23
Kin 90

Wednesday **MARCH**
29

MARCH Thursday

30

day 24
Kin 91

MARCH Friday

31

day 25
Kin 92

APRIL Saterday

1

day 26
Kin 93
GAP

APRIL Sunday

2

day 27
Kin 94

"Once upon a time there was no time."
- anonymous -

April 4 - May 1
Totem animal: Dog
Dominant Tone: Tone 10 - produce, perfect, manifestation

Manifestation

Finally the time has come. You are ready to realize your purpose and to manifest it here on Earth. It is no longer something that just took shape in your mind, you can now actually touch it. It becomes reality on this planet. That's why we call it Planetary Moon. However, before you get ready, it is wise to include your intention and consideration of the 9th Moon. It might be wise to change it a little here and there. Perfect before you manifest.

Dog

The Dog is the 10th Seal and this is the 10th Moon. The Dog plays an important role in myths and legends in many tribes all over the world. The Maya recognized an enormous dog in the starry sky including the sign of Aries and Taurus. His tail went as far as Cetus (Whale). The Maya called this Dog 'Pek'.

The key words for the Dog are love and loyalty. This month you are asked to perform your actions from the heart. If you don't do that, your action will miss its purpose and nobody will enjoy it. Is it really what you had in mind when you set your purpose? Does it give you the pleasure and satisfaction you expected? Or does it need some more perfection? Or do you have to let go of the idea that it has to be perfect before you actually manifest? After all, the urge for perfection can hamper your joy of life.

The Dog is an excellent guide, that's why people use guide dogs. Whenever you feel you may have lost your way, call upon the power of the Dog. The Aztecs used to sacrifice a dog and to bury it with the deceased, so it would guide him through the Underworld. The Dog is also an excellent guard. Even asleep, he will hear every sound and he will guard his territory against intruders. This month you will be asked to take a good look at the borders of your territory. Are there any intruders who need to be growled and barked at? Being loyal to yourself sometimes means being very clear to others. Don't hesitate to show your teeth from time to time.

In the glyph of Dog, the ears are sometimes presented as breasts. The dog then represents all mammals; it is the ability to nurse and to maintain relationship with other kin.

The first day of the Moon = 5 Warrior
When you ask yourself the question how you can perfect what you are doing, you may include the energy of the Uppertone Warrior. It is the energy of the Empowerment of Intelligence. Maybe you can show just how well you have thought your manifestation over...

Human Wavespell
Man has Free Will, but do you really want to choose? In the western world, freedom of choice has become a burden. What do I want to eat? What newspaper do I want to read? Whom do I want to see? Where do I want to go? There is so much choice, we often end up in 'who, what, where, which' too soon, skipping the first question: "Do I want to...?" Ask yourself what it is you really want.
The Solar Seal Human also represents teeth: take well care of your teeth. Pay attention these 13 days to whether or not (and if so, how?) others are trying to influence you. Also pay attention to whether or not you yourself are trying to influence others.

Serpent Wavespell
You may have noticed that the Serpent Wavespell has many GAPs: Galactic Activation Portals. These are intensive days, in which many things can be transformed. It requires a strong focus. The Serpent represents ancient energy, flowing from the Earth up your spine. Your body is the tube, the entrance to the cosmos. Are you comfortable in your body? Does the energy flow without obstructions? Where are your blockades? What is causing them? These days can be filled with extremes: Serpent is both poisonous and base, and it is the symbol of advanced medicine.

Mirror Wavespell
Part of this Wavespell we are in the middle column of the Tzolkin, where future and past join and are reflected in the present. The seal for Mirror is like the Tzolkin. They both looks like a sand-glass. Imagine the pressure at the point where the sand passes the middle. Indeed! It is an intensive period, that will make your heart beat faster and your blood pressure go up. Take extra care if yourself this period.
Mirror reflects. You might be hurt by the shadow side of some people, as they try to pin their problems onto you. Don't be fooled. Search for the truth. In some occasions it will be sufficient to mirror them, to give their problems back to them, where they belong. And naturally, you ask yourself the question whether or not you pin something onto someone else...

notes

day 28
Kin 95

Monday **APRIL**
3

Red week of initiation
day 1 *Planetary Dog Moon*
Kin 96
GAP

Tuesday **APRIL**
4

day 2
Kin 97

Wednesday **APRIL**
5

APRIL Thursday

6

day 3
Kin 98

APRIL Friday

7

day 4
Kin 99

APRIL Saterday

8

day 5
Kin 100

APRIL Sunday

9

day 6
Kin 101

"When I was born I was so surprised I didn't talk for a year and a half."
- Gracie Allen (1906 - 1964) -

notes

day 7
Kin 102

Monday **APRIL**

10

White week of refinement
Tuesday **APRIL**

day 8
Kin 103

11

day 9
Kin 104

Wednesday **APRIL**

12

APRIL Thursday

13

day 10
Kin 105

●

APRIL Friday

14   Good Friday

day 11 ⊠
Kin 106
GAP

●●

APRIL Saterday

15

day 12
Kin 107
GAP

●●●

APRIL Sunday

16   Easter Sunday

day 13
Kin 108
GAP

●●●●

"Creativity is allowing yourself to make mistakes. Art is knowing which ones to keep."
- Scott Adams - 12 Skywalker

notes

day 14
Kin 109
GAP

Monday **APRIL**

Easter Monday **17**

Blue week of transformation

day 15
Kin 110
GAP

Tuesday **APRIL**

18

day 16
Kin 111
GAP

Wednesday **APRIL**

19

Yellow Cosmic Seed Year
Planetary Dog Moon

APRIL Thursday
20

day 17
Kin 112
GAP

APRIL Friday
21

day 18
Kin 113
GAP

APRIL Saterday
22

day 19
Kin 114
GAP

APRIL Sunday
23

day 20
Kin 115
GAP

"The greatest gifts you can give your children are the roots of responsibility and the wings of independence."
- Denis Waitley -

notes

 day 21
Kin 116

Monday **APRIL**

24

 **day 22**
Kin 117

Yellow week of ripening
Tuesday **APRIL**

25

day 23
Kin 118

Wednesday **APRIL**

26

APRIL Thursday

27

day 24

Kin 119 ○ ○

APRIL Friday

28

day 25

Kin 120 ○ ○ ○

APRIL Saterday

29

day 26

Kin 121 ○ ○ ○ ○

APRIL Sunday

30

day 27

Kin 122

"Life is not measured by the breaths we take, but by the moments that take our breath away."
- George Carlin - 13 Moon

Spectral Serpent Moon

May 2 - May 29
Totem animal: Serpent
Dominant Tone: Tone 11 - release, dissolve, liberation

Serpent

We don't need to wonder why the Serpent is the totem animal of the Spectral Moon of Liberation. The Serpent effortlessly leaves his skin behind so he can continue fully reborn.

The Serpent was the most sacred animal of the Maya, together with the Jaguar. Quetzalcoatl, the Feathered Serpent, was the main God of the Aztecs and the Toltecs. This God is often represented as an upright Serpent (Coatl in the language of the Aztecs), with the beautiful green-blue feathers of the Quetzal bird. He was a deity who - according to legend - truly existed. This divine Serpent descended from Heaven on Earth in order to found a state. He lived a sober life, withdrawn like a priest. He was seduced to a hallucinatory drink and made love with the demonic Goddess of the Mushroom. He subsequently left Earth in a ship made of snake skin, ashamed of what he had done. The rising sun set fire to his ship and his heart flew back to the heavens.

Quetzalcoatl is associated with Venus as the morning star. He is also associated with the Lord of the Winds, who gave life with his breath. This might explain the connection with the Solar Seal Wind, represented as the letter T: symbol of the rattle of a rattlesnake. The rattle can be found high in the sky in the Pleiades.

Release

Personally, I see yet another connection between the Serpent and 'release', in the sense of 'putting into this world'. Once I stayed with friends on a farm. Early in the morning I walked through the garden to a vast pasture, to see the morning haze rise. Still half asleep I stretched out and bowed down to the ground to stretch my legs. With my curls hanging down, I suddenly saw something move. Something was curling, like the curls of my hair. First I just saw one of them, then another one, and yet another one. They were little snakes. My head looked like the head of Medusa! I was startled and got up to check my vision. With my sleepy curly head, I had been hanging upside down in a grass snake's nest, right at the time the babies came out of their eggs. I remembered seeing two large grass snakes earlier that year, living in the dung-hill. It was a magnificent sight: all those baby snakes shooting away from the center, starting a life of their own. What a powerful image: 'releasing', setting free and moving into the world.

That's why this 11th Moon represents letting go and putting into the world whatever it is you manifested during the 10th Moon. Let it live a life of its own, let it follow its own cycle. Feel how free you are from your task. It's done!

Mirror Wavespell

Part of this Wavespell we are in the middle column of the Tzolkin, where future and past join and are reflected in the present. The seal for Mirror is like the Tzolkin. They both looks like a sand-glass. Imagine the pressure at the point where the sand passes the middle. Indeed! It is an intensive period, that will make your heart beat faster and your blood pressure go up. Take extra care if yourself this period.

Mirror reflects. You might be hurt by the shadow side of some people, as they try to pin their problems onto you. Don't be fooled. Search for the truth. In some occasions it will be sufficient to mirror them, to give their problems back to them, where they belong. And naturally, you ask yourself the question whether or not you pin something onto someone else...

Monkey Wavespell

We are still in the middle column of the Tzolkin. As a matter of fact, this Wavespell begins right in the center of the calendar. This is where we are closest to Hunab K'u, the source of all life. Many things happen that could make you very serious. Too serious even. If there is a way to please God it will be by happiness and laughter. Use Monkey's sense of humor, dare to play and become invincible. Be the light-hearted, spontaneous child. But, stay on the alert, or Monkey will fool you. It is now time to liberate the Inner Child and transform the shadows from your childhood, but only by remaining in the Here and Now.

Seed Wavespell

Seed is where all talents and abilities meet. What do you need to let that Seed germinate? This Wavespell in this Moon, it is time to liberate and fully life your sexuality and creativity. Is there something obstructing you, preventing you to fully developing. Could it be your own judgment? Ideas such as "There's no way I could ever do that!", "It's filthy to sweat" or "I will never be the best" will obstruct the germination of Seed. Liberate yourself! Seed wants to sprout! And don't be too impatient, that too is part of the Seed Wavespell.

notes

day 28
Kin 123

Monday **MAY**

1

Red week of initiation
Tuesday **MAY**

day 1 *Spectral Serpent Moon*
Kin 124

2

day 2
Kin 125

Wednesday **MAY**

3

MAY Thursday

4

day 3
Kin 126

MAY Friday

5

day 4
Kin 127

MAY Saterday

6

day 5
Kin 128

MAY Sunday

7

day 6
Kin 129

*"When you start using senses you've neglected,
your reward is to see the world with completely fresh eyes."
- Barbara Sher - 3 Wind*

notes

○○○ **day 7**
Kin 130

Monday **MAY**

8

White week of refinement
Tuesday **MAY**

day 8
Kin 131

9

•• **day 9**
Kin 132

Wednesday **MAY**

10

MAY Thursday

11

day 10
Kin 133 • • •

MAY Friday

12

day 11
Kin 134 • • • •

MAY Saterday

13

day 12
Kin 135

MAY Sunday

14

day 13
Kin 136 •

"I have no special talent. I am only passionately curious."
- Albert Einstein - 13 Sun

notes

day 14
Kin 137

Monday **MAY**
15

Blue week of transformation

day 15
Kin 138

Tuesday **MAY**
16

day 16
Kin 139

Wednesday **MAY**
17

MAY Thursday

18

day 17
Kin 140

MAY Friday

19

day 18
Kin 141

MAY Saterday

20

day 19
Kin 142

MAY Sunday

21

day 20
Kin 143

*"The talent for being happy is appreciating and liking what you have,
instead of what you don't have."*
- Woody Allen - 9 Mirror

notes

---

day 21
Kin 144

Monday **MAY**

22

Yellow week of ripening

day 22
Kin 145

Tuesday **MAY**

23

---

day 23
Kin 146
GAP

Wednesday **MAY**

24

MAY Thursday

25

day 24
Kin 147
GAP

MAY Friday

26

day 25
Kin 148
GAP

MAY Saterday

27

day 26
Kin 149
GAP

MAY Sunday

28

day 27
Kin 150
GAP

"Even if you are a minority of one, the truth is the truth."
- Gandhi - 10 Human

May 30 - June 26
Totem animal: Rabbit
Dominant Tone: Tone 12 - universalize, dedicate, cooperation

Universalize

After having manifested your purpose during the 10th Moon (or having 'given birth to your child') and after having let go of that purpose during the 11th Moon (or 'let your child breathe on its own'), you now (during the 12th Moon) take a good look at what it is it needs. Give it shelter and a roof above its head. What does it need to take its position in this world? Universalize it. That is this Moon's task. This is what you will dedicate yourself to.

Cooperation

Now you can watch and see how your manifestation relates to the rest. How does it cooperate? This is also a good Moon to get together with other people. It is a time to evaluate. There were 12 knights of the Round Table and Jesus had 12 disciples. Look at the previous Moons. What has been done and how did it go?

Rabbit

Ixchel or Ixquic was the Moon Goddess of the Maya. She is often represented with a rabbit in her arms. Young Ixquic and her son Ixbalanqué often appeared to people as rabbits and hares. In the dark spots on the moon, the Maya recognized the profile of a rabbit. That's why rabbits are Moon animals. They were worshiped by the Maya for their astuteness and their courage. Quite likely, the deed of the Rabbit in the myth of the heroic twins Hunahpú and Ixbalanqué is linked to this courage. When Hunahpú was decapitated by the lords of the Underworld, and his head was exhibited at the place of the ball games, Ixbalanqué made a pumpkin to replace the head of his brother. He asked the Rabbit to sit in a tree, close to the place of the ball games. During the ball game, he shot the ball in the direction of the Rabbit. As agreed, the Rabbit ran away, followed by the Lords of the Underworld. Ixbalanqué used this moment to replace his brother's head by the pumpkin. That's how Hunahpú was saved. This is the courageous deed of the Rabbit that is referred to. In our culture, the rabbit is often seen as a fearful being, that freezes when danger appears. He waits before he reacts and runs. But in the story of Alice in Wonderland, it was the rabbit who guided her to the world of magic via holes and tunnels. The Maya called the rabbit 'Tzub'. The star system Rabbit can be found between the rattle of the Serpent and the Turtle. Aldebaran (another star) was his eye.

Crystal-clear
The rabbit has big eyes in the sides of his head. This enables him to have a panorama view of almost 360 degrees, seeing just about everything. He can almost see what's behind him and he can look straight up. The eyes of a rabbit work like a crystal, bundling all the light signals. Be like the Rabbit: let all points of view come together, then everything will become crystal-clear!

Seed Wavespell
Seed is where all talents and abilities meet. What do you need to let that Seed germinate? This Wavespell in this Moon, it is time to liberate and fully life your sexuality and creativity. Is there something obstructing you, preventing you to fully developing. Could it be your own judgment? Ideas such as "There's no way I could ever do that!", "It's filthy to sweat" or "I will never be the best" will obstruct the germination of Seed. Liberate yourself! Seed wants to sprout! And don't be too impatient, that too is part of the Seed Wavespell.

Earth Wavespell
What new thread is evolving in your life? Can you see how your path is connected to the Universe? Don't hesitate to follow.
Stubbornness may be in your way, these 13 days. You might meet people who are totally convinced of their own ideas and who refuse to let go of them. Are they reflecting what you are doing yourself? Use the absorbing quality of Mother Earth to let this stubbornness flow into her. Earth will transform your suspicion into faith and she will remind you of your path. Earthquakes may appear out of nowhere, causing major shifts in your work or in your personal life.

Dog Wavespell
The Dog is about faith and loyalty, about guiding and being guided. What is it that guides you? Is it good for you? Do you refuse to see something in order to avoid a confrontation? Be in charge of your own life and be loyal to your ideals. What is it you long for? What makes your heart sing? The Mayan word for dog also means feet. Pay attention to your feet, so you don't stub your toe. Feet might very well mean 'to follow' or 'to stand with both feet on the ground'.

Yellow Cosmic Seed Year

Crystal Rabbit Moon

notes

---

day 28
Kin 151
GAP

Monday **MAY**
29

Red week of initiation
day 1 *Crystal Rabbit Moon*
Kin 152
GAP

Tuesday **MAY**
30

---

day 2
Kin 153
GAP

Wednesday **MAY**
31

JUNE Thursday

1

day 3
Kin 154
GAP

JUNE Friday

2

day 4
Kin 155
GAP

JUNE Saterday

3

day 5
Kin 156

JUNE Sunday

4

day 6
Kin 157

*"Forget not that the earth delights to feel your bare feet
and the winds long to play with your hair."
- Kahlil Gibran - 7 Earth*

notes

day 7
Kin 158

Monday **JUNE**

5

White week of refinement
day 8
Kin 159

Tuesday **JUNE**

6

day 9
Kin 160

Wednesday **JUNE**

7

JUNE Thursday

8

day 10

Kin 161

JUNE Friday

9

day 11

Kin 162

JUNE Saterday

10

day 12

Kin 163

JUNE Sunday

11

day 13

Kin 164

*"Even if I knew that tomorrow the world would go to pieces,
I would still plant my apple tree."
- Martin Luther King Jr. - 5 Human*

notes

 day 14
Kin 165
GAP

Monday **JUNE**
12

Blue week of transformation
Tuesday **JUNE**
13

day 15
Kin 166

day 16
Kin 167

Wednesday **JUNE**
14

JUNE Thursday
15

day 17
Kin 168
GAP

JUNE Friday
16

day 18
Kin 169

JUNE Saterday
17

day 19
Kin 170

○

JUNE Sunday
18

day 20
Kin 171

○ ○

---

*"Play is, in fact, one of the most practical methods of survival, both individually
and for the species. Within its framework lies the secrets of creativity,
and within the secrets of creativity lie the secrets of being."*
- Jane Roberts -

notes

○○○ **day 21**
Kin 172

Monday **JUNE**
19

Yellow week of ripening

○○○○ **day 22**
Kin 173
GAP

Tuesday **JUNE**
20

— **day 23**
Kin 174

Wednesday **JUNE**

Summer solstice **21**
726 AM EST
- 1226 GMT

JUNE Thursday

22

day 24
Kin 175

JUNE Friday

23

day 25
Kin 176
GAP

JUNE Saterday

24

day 26
Kin 177

JUNE Sunday

25

day 27
Kin 178

"There are two ways of spreading light - to be the candle or the mirror that reflects it."
- Edith Wharton -

June 27 - July 24
Totem animal: Turtle
Dominant Tone: Tone 13 - transcend, endure, presence

Turtle
This last Moon is a good Moon to think about this year and to rest. Nothing must be done, everything is allowed. The Turtle ('Aak' in the Mayan language) was known for her old age and her patience. That's why she suits this last Moon of the year. Legend has it that the Turtle and the Tree are the wisest grandchildren of Grandmother Galaxy, for they were initiated into the Knowledge of Time for all living beings on Mother Earth. A Turtle carries the Knowledge of Time on her shell. The inner shell consists of 13 sections, like the 13 Moons of the year. The outer shell consists of 28 sections, the number of days in a month. Yet also in many other cultures, the Turtle is considered a sacred animal, due to her unique qualities: the Turtle is always home, since she carries her house on her back. She is not bound to certain places. She feels at home both in the water and ashore. When there is danger she pulls her head inside her shell, but she also knows that she will have to reach out her neck in order to make her way in this world.

Mayahuel is the Mayan Goddess of Nourishment and Fertility. She is represented in a bearing position, leaning on a turtle. She is the protector

of the womb where all life comes from. That's why she was also called Ayopechtli: 'sitting on a turtle'. The sweat lodge represents both the womb and the Turtle.

Endure

The Native Americans referred to their land as "Turtle Island". Turtle Island is the surface of the earth before it was separated into the continents as we know them today. Legend has it that, when the first conflicts arose between men, Great Mystery decided to purify the Earth with water. The sole survivors after the Great Flood were a man, a few animals and some birds. The man just floated there, all by himself in the great ocean, holding on to a trunk. The Turtle saw the poor man's situation and let him sit on her back. That's how the Turtle became a home for all that lives.

That is precisely what this last Moon of the year asks of you: to be compassionate with every living being and to offer help. Let everything be, in full presence, from a state of inner peace. And with a smile on your face, as the Buddhists say...

Dog Wavespell

Dog is about faith and loyalty, about guiding and being guided. What is it that guides you? Is it good for you? Do you refuse to see something in order to avoid a confrontation? Be in charge of your own life and be loyal to your ideals. What is it you long for? What makes your heart sing? The Mayan word for dog also means feet. Pay attention to your feet, so you don't stub your toe. Feet might very well mean 'to follow' or 'to stand with both feet on the ground'.

Night Wavespell

Summer time is tempting you to be busy with all kinds of activities. But the Night Wavespell is asking you to focus on the inner self. These days you might feel more tired than usual. Go to bed if you want to, it's Dream Time! Write down your dreams. Housing issues might ask your attention these 13 days. If so, give it your attention. This could also be your inner house. Do you feel at home in and with yourself? In the Dream World there is no shortage. Fear of shortage is the opposite of abundance. Don't be tempted to fall back into your fears. The Wavespell challenges you; keep the faith!

Warrior Wavespell

Temptation is near in the shape of beautiful things; you are especially drawn to shining things! It is the Warrior, the Crow and the Vulture in you that make you greedy. Don't be seduced, ask questions instead. Do I really need that? Will that make me happy? Clarify your motivations. You may be a bit confused these days, due to all this questioning. Nothing seems obvious anymore. Be without fear, for it is quite a special state of being when nothing is certain anymore. Enjoy it and don't be too serious. Remember it is the last Moon of the year; time to rest and throttle down.

notes

day 28
Kin 179

Monday **JUNE**

26

day 1 Cosmic Turtle Moon
Kin 180

Red week of initiation
Tuesday **JUNE**

27

day 2
Kin 181

Wednesday **JUNE**

28

Cosmic Turtle Moon

JUNE Thursday

29

day 3

Kin 182

JUNE Friday

30

day 4

Kin 183

JULY Saterday

1

day 5

Kin 184

GAP

JULY Sunday

2

day 6

Kin 185

---

*"Think of the magic of that foot, comparatively small, upon which your whole weight rests.
It's a miracle, and the dance is a celebration of that miracle."*
- Martha Graham - 8 Skywalker

Yellow Cosmic Seed Year

Cosmic Turtle Moon

JUN 27 - JUL 24, 2006

notes

---

day 7
Kin 186

Monday **JULY**

3

White week of refinement

day 8
Kin 187

Tuesday **JULY**

4

---

day 9
Kin 188

Wednesday **JULY**

5

Yellow Cosmic Seed Year
Cosmic Turtle Moon

JULY Thursday

6

day 10
Kin 189
GAP

JULY Friday

7

day 11
Kin 190

JULY Saterday

8

day 12
Kin 191

JULY Sunday

9

day 13
Kin 192
GAP

"The art of being wise is the art of knowing what to overlook."
- William James - 5 Skywalker

notes

---

day 14
Kin 193

Monday **JULY**

10

Blue week of transformation

day 15
Kin 194

Tuesday **JULY**

11

---

day 16
Kin 195

Wednesday **JULY**

12

JULY Thursday
13

day 17
Kin 196

JULY Friday
14

day 18
Kin 197
GAP

JULY Saterday
15

day 19
Kin 198

JULY Sunday
16

day 20
Kin 199

*"It takes a real storm in the average person's life to make him realize how much
worrying he has done over the squalls."*
- Bruce Barton - 8 Storm

notes

day 21
Kin 200

Monday **JULY**

17

day 22
Kin 201

Yellow week of ripening
Tuesday **JULY**

18

day 23
Kin 202

Wednesday **JULY**

19

JULY Thursday

20

day 24
Kin 203
GAP

JULY Friday

21

day 25
Kin 204

JULY Saterday

22

day 26
Kin 205

JULY Sunday

23

day 27
Kin 206

"Alles was entsteht, ist wert dass es zu grunde geht."
- Johann Wolfgang von Goethe - 13 Skywalker

notes

 day 28
Kin 207

Monday **JULY**
24

Day out of Time
Kin 208

Tuesday **JULY**
25

Day out of Time

13 Moons of 28 days make 364 days. The one day left is the Day out of Time, celebrated each year on July 25. In the 13-Moon Calendar, July 26 is the first day of the new year. July 25 is the day in between two years, a Day out of Time. It's a day on which connections are made: the old is let go of and the intention for the following year is set. It is a day of being conscious.

The Day out of Time is the 'Galactic Be In', when we celebrate that we are all artists, co-creators of the One Creation as Galactic beings, living as human beings on Earth, together with the four-legged ones, the winged ones, the crawling ones, the finned ones of the waters, the standing ones, the stone people, the plants, the water, air and fire.

This day is a day for peace and culture and is celebrated all over the world. Many thousands of people get together through the power of love and telepathy, in order to let our human culture bloom in harmony with the Earth.

July 25, 2006 - Yellow Cosmic Star
Endure elegance by transcendence and beautification. Be Art! This is the day for peace and culture. Make everything beautiful, colorful and elegant. Party, celebrate that you are!

Visit www.tortuga.com to see whether any feasts are being organized in your vicinity, or be creative and organize your own feast. And you can do the Rainbow Bridge Meditation, download at www.lawoftime.org/law/rainbow.html

Happy New
Red Magnetic Moon Year

1 Moon Year

Red Magnetic Moon Year - Mayan name: Hun Muluc

	Action	**Power**	**Function**
1	Attract	Unite	Purpose
Moon	Purify	Universal water	Flow

Combining these keys, one gets:

> *Unite universal water,*
> *by attracting and purifying,*
> *creating the purpose of/to flow.*

The energy of the Moon seal always deals with feelings and emotions. The Moon is all the water: the seas, the rivers, the water in your body, the water in the womb, your tears, your sweat. You need this water to survive. By means of these fluids, infinite pulses in your brains are being sent through your body to your muscles and organs, and vice versa. Water makes us fertile; without it we would dehydrate and die. 'Uniting universal water in order to attract and purify' means lots of tears, emotions, sweat, drinking water to kick off all the processes in your body, as a new start of a 13-year cycle. Moon is the power of re-collection. We can feel right through people and situations, if our Moon body flows well. We know what is true and what is false. It makes us sensitive, without being emotional. We function like an antenna that receives even all the unspoken words. The Red Magnetic Moon Year could be the year in which we start communicating with each other in a different, much more sensitive way. It is no longer just a few individuals who understand and are able to do this. The paranormal becomes normal.

Magnetic Bat Moon

July 26 - August 22
Totem animal: Bat
Dominant tone: Tone 1 - attract, unify, purpose

The Bat

The Bat symbolizes Rebirth. Hanging upside down in a dark cave, he reflects the position of a baby in the womb before being born. The power of the Bat was highly respected by the Aztecs, the Toltecs and the Maya. Even today, a group of people called the Tzotziles (Bat People) live in Chiapas, Mexico. The Bat gives us strength for a shaman death; the power to let your old Self die and to let go of all your ideas about yourself, that will keep you separated from your soul path. Only then will you be able to focus on your purpose, like a new-born child.

How to use your time; determine a purpose in 4 weeks

This is the first Moon of the new year, and the start of a new cycle of 13 Moons. During this first month, you may give this year a purpose. You have 28 days to do so, which is good, for determining a purpose is not a small thing. The energy of this year is to 'unite universal water' (see year description), like the blowing wind. It will be wise to let your personal purpose ride on the wings of this wind. The 13-Moon Calendar can be of service in yet another way. When you take a look at the weeks of the Moons, you will see that each week has its own color. (Colored lines above the days). You can use this every Moon. This Moon you can let your purpose arise in 4 phases: 4 weeks of 7 days. The first red week of initiation will show you your possible desires, for your purpose will be born from these desires. It is useless defining a purpose if it isn't a reflection of your deepest desires. How could you continue for 13 Moons if you don't really long for it?
So how do you find out what it is you really desire? Maybe you have hidden your desires under many layers of practical goals and social interests, or limitations

such as finding a new job, paying more attention to your weight, quitting smoking. This doesn't make your heart sing though, does it? You will find it easy to recognize your true heart's desire: your heart will start beating faster while thinking about this desire. If that is the case, you know you're on the right track! All you have to do then is to accept this desire instead of pushing it away as 'impossible'. Acceptance of your desire unites inside and outside.

The second white week of refinement is there to refine your purpose. Write down your desire every single day, until the words come from your soul. This is your correct description. Be aware not to be guided by negative thoughts and insecurities about yourself, such as "There's no way I can do that!".

Use the power of the Bat; let go of old ideas about yourself and grant yourself a new chance!

The third blue week of transformation is about collecting or attracting energy necessary to transform your desire into purpose.

The fourth week is the yellow week of ripening. Your purpose becomes clear; you carry it as a true part of yourself. At the end of this month you will no longer be able to picture yourself without this purpose.

Image of the Bat as the 'uinal' Zoth, a month of 20 days in the original Maya Calendar. Zoth means BAT.

Moon Wavespell

Moon deals with feelings and emotions. Moon is universal water: the seas, rivers, the water in your body, the water of the womb, your tears, your sweat. All life needs water. During the Moon Wavespell you may lose it emotionally, with many tears, rage and dramatic behavior. And not just you, so beware! It is wise to purify your body with water. Visit a sauna to sweat, drink a lot of water. Make sure all processes can flow freely through your body. Moon is the power of remembrance. With a well flowing Moon body you will be able to easily feel through people and situations. You know what is true and what is false. You are like an antenna that receives the unspoken words.

Wind Wavespell

These 13 days misunderstandings are just around the corner. You will need to give extra attention to communication. Try to speak clearly and honestly. This Moon year you will hear the unspoken words. Ask questions about it. Is it true? Communicate!

Try to be fully aware of your breathing. What is it you breathe in? In what rhythm? Sacrifice your breath as a gift to the Great Spirit/Hunab K'u, then all your words will flow in this stream. When God created man, he blew life into him with his own breath. Breathe in this Spirit and Inspiration will await you.

Eagle Wavespell

During the Eagle Wavespell your responsibilities may be pointed out to you. The more you try to escape from them, the more Eagle will fly after you and grab you with his strong claws. His action may seem rough, but didn't you see the web you were caught in? It is for your own good. Eagle asks you to fly with him and to take a look at your own life. See where you are and determine where you want to go. Take a little distance, take a good look and - if necessary - change your direction.

notes

My purpose for this year is:

purpose

day 1 Magnetic Bat Moon
Kin 209

Red week of initiation
Wednesday **JULY**

26

JULY Thursday
27

day 2
Kin 210
GAP

• •

JULY Friday
28

day 3
Kin 211
GAP

• • •

JULY Saterday
29

day 4
Kin 212

• • • •

JULY Sunday
30

day 5
Kin 213

—

"The voyage of discovery lies not in finding new landscapes but in having new eyes."
- Marcel Proust - 6 Seed

notes

 day 6
Kin 214

Monday **JULY**
31

 day 7
Kin 215

Tuesday **AUGUST**
1

White week of refinement
Wednesday **AUGUST**
2

 day 8
Kin 216

AUGUST Thursday

3

day 9
Kin 217

••••

AUGUST Friday

4

day 10
Kin 218
GAP

‗‗

AUGUST Saterday

5

day 11
Kin 219

•
‗‗

AUGUST Sunday

6

day 12
Kin 220

••
‗‗

"When we let our own light shine, we unconsciously give other people permission to do the same."
- Marianne Williamson - 7 Dragon

Red Magnetic Moon Year
Magnetic Bat Moon

JUL 26 - AUG 22, 2006

notes

---

day 13
Kin 221

Monday **AUGUST**

7

---

day 14
Kin 222
GAP

Tuesday **AUGUST**

8

Blue week of transformation
Wednesday **AUGUST**

day 15
Kin 223

9

AUGUST Thursday

10

day 16

Kin 224   ○ ○ ○

AUGUST Friday

11

day 17

Kin 225 ○ ○ ○ ○

AUGUST Saterday

12

day 18

Kin 226 ⎯

AUGUST Sunday

13

day 19

Kin 227 ○ ⎯

"Understanding can overcome any situation, however mysterious or insurmountable it may appear to be."
- Norman Vincent Peale - 6 Skywalker

notes

---

day 20
Kin 228

Monday **AUGUST**

14

---

day 21
Kin 229

Tuesday **AUGUST**

15

Yellow week of ripening
Wednesday **AUGUST**

day 22
Kin 230

16

AUGUST Thursday

17

day 23

Kin 231

AUGUST Friday

18

day 24

Kin 232

AUGUST Saterday

19

day 25

Kin 233

AUGUST Sunday

20

day 26

Kin 234

---

*"I believe in everything until it's disproved. So I believe in fairies, the myths, dragons.
It all exists, even if it's in your mind. Who's to say that dreams and nightmares
aren't as real as the here and now?"*
- John Lennon - 10 Wizard

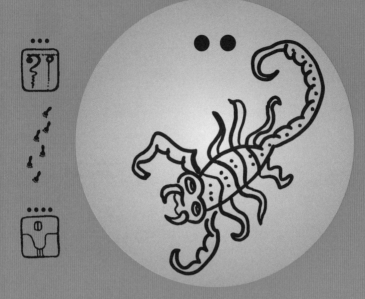

August 23 - September 19
Totem animal: Scorpion
Dominant Tone: Tone 2 - stabilize, polarize, challenge

This Moon contains a polarizing power. Polarity means opposite; North and South
are the opposite poles of the Earth. They are two sides of the same, fully related
to each other. One would not exist without the other. There is no light without
shadow. Lunar comes from Luna (Moon). Mother Moon shows us her polarity: we
can only see her from one side. If we look only superficially and we forget the
other side, we would forget that she is a beautiful sphere.

You can experience the polarizing energy of this Moon/month in various ways.
You can consciously focus on the other side (the shadow side). We often, however,
focus on the one side (the light), trying to get away from the other side (darkness).
Yet it is those features of yourself you want to get away from, that took you to
great heights. This is where you can find your motivation for growth, this is what
gives you energy. It is by facing your shadow side that your soul can grow! This
is your stimulus and your challenge.

Tone 2 asks you to lovingly look at your other side, your shadow side, since
this is what moves you, what challenges you. Thus, embrace your shadow as
stimulating growth for your soul!

Scorpion

During this Moon you can count on your shadow side to suddenly reveal itself.
The polarizing power of the Lunar Scorpion Moon is as unpredictable as a
scorpion. You never know when they cross your path and sting. The shadow side
of you and of other people might quite suddenly pop around the corner. When that
happens, it is your task to keep an eye on the whole. The action that accompanies

this Moon is 'to stabilize'. Don't be tempted into fighting shadow with shadow. Send light and love. That is your challenge.

Stabilize

In the annual Wavespell - the process of 13 steps - you defined your purpose during the first Moon. During the second Moon you take a look at what keeps you away from your purpose. What is my challenge? What obstacles lie on my path? Step 2 stabilizes the positive energy of the enthusiasm, created by the kick-off of a new project. Don't take action just yet. Don't be tempted to get rid of the obstacles. You can do that later. First collect the means.

Scorpion Goddess

Eagle Wavespell

During the Eagle Wavespell your responsibilities may be pointed out to you. The more you try to escape from them, the more Eagle will fly after you and grab you with his strong claws. His action may seem rough, but didn't you see the web you were caught in? It is for your own good. Eagle asks you to fly with him and to take a look at your own life. See where you are and determine where you want to go. Take a little distance, take a good look and - if necessary - change your direction.

Star Wavespell

This is the last Wavespell of the Tzolkin and for a good reason! This is where you can perfect things. Finish your creation, so that it becomes a work of Art. Star's shadow is resistance: something your will both encounter and search for these days. You will be focused on your environment and not be in touch much with your inner world. It is wise to radiate inside from time to time, to create enlightenment there as well! Remember that maybe the Star can only be found on the scorpions tail; go into the darkness, because it has to be dark enough, to see the stars (see quote Ralph Waldo Emerson).

Dragon Wavespell

Man has a tendency to control, change or improve his environment. This Wavespell is about letting things be the way they are. Do not complain when it rains, but cherish the wet drops falling on your head. Do not get upset in traffic. It is the way it is. Be like a tree that watches the world around it, free of judgement and without wanting to change anything. Cherish life just the way it is. Be your own mother and give yourself what it is you truly need. Cherish your belly and your womb as the source of all life.

notes

---

day 27
Kin 235

Monday **AUGUST**

21

---

day 28
Kin 236

Tuesday **AUGUST**

22

---

day 1 *Lunar Scorpion Moon*
Kin 237

Red week of initiation
Wednesday **AUGUST**

23

AUGUST Thursday

24

day 2
Kin 238

····

AUGUST Friday

25

day 3
Kin 239
GAP

●

AUGUST Saterday

26

day 4
Kin 240

•

AUGUST Sunday

27

day 5
Kin 241
GAP

••

"If you nurture your mind, body, and spirit, your time will expand.
You will gain a new perspective that will allow you to accomplish much more."
- Brian Koslow -

Red Magnetic Moon Year
Lunar Scorpion Moon

AUG 23 - SEP 19, 2006

notes

• • •
〔⌡〕 **day 6**
〔♉〕 Kin 242

Monday **AUGUST**
28

• • • •
day 7
Kin 243

Tuesday **AUGUST**
29

= =
day 8
Kin 244

White week of refinement
Wednesday **AUGUST**
30

AUGUST Thursday

31

day 9
Kin 245

SEPTEMBER Friday

1

day 10
Kin 246

SEPTEMBER Saterday

2

day 11
Kin 247

SEPTEMBER Sunday

3

day 12
Kin 248

"When it is dark enough, you can see the stars."
- Ralph Waldo Emerson - 9 Human (guide = Star)

notes

day 13
Kin 249

Monday **SEPTEMBER**

4

day 14
Kin 250

Tuesday **SEPTEMBER**

5

Blue week of transformation

day 15
Kin 251

Wednesday **SEPTEMBER**

6

SEPTEMBER Thursday

7

day 16

Kin 252

SEPTEMBER Friday

8

day 17

Kin 253

SEPTEMBER Saterday

9

day 18

Kin 254

SEPTEMBER Sunday

10

day 19

Kin 255

---

*"Your vision will become clear only when you can look into your own heart.
Who looks outside, dreams; who looks inside, awakes."*
- Carl G. Jung - 13 Wizard

notes

day 20
Kin 256

Monday **SEPTEMBER**
11

day 21
Kin 257

Tuesday **SEPTEMBER**
12

Yellow week of ripening

day 22
Kin 258

Wednesday **SEPTEMBER**
13

SEPTEMBER Thursday
14

day 23
Kin 259

SEPTEMBER Friday
15

day 24
Kin 260
GAP

SEPTEMBER Saterday
16

day 25
Kin 1, first day of the Tzolkin
GAP

SEPTEMBER Sunday
17

day 26
Kin 2

---

*"Who has seen the wind? Neither you nor I but when the trees bow down their heads,
the wind is passing by."*
- Christina Rossetti - 9 Dragon

Electric Deer Moon

September 20 - October 17
Totem animal: Deer
Dominant Tone: Tone 3 - bond, activate, service

Deer

The deer was very important to the Maya. The Thunder God Tohil appeared as a white deer and brought along the masculine power of creation and fathering: the activating aspect of this Moon. The Moon Goddess Ixchel (or Ixquic as she was called as well) gave herself in total surrender to Tohil as a red deer. The feminine deer represents surrender, reception and unconscious powers.

The similarity between the English 'deer' and 'dear' (in Dutch 'hert' and 'hart') is not a coincidence. The deer teaches us to use the power of gentleness and care to touch the hearts and souls of all wounded beings who try to keep us away from our path. Be prepared to love yourself and others as they are, and your fears and obstacles will simply melt away. Be gentle to yourself and to your negativity. Connect via your heart. Love is the key that connects everything.

There are many images of Mayan Gods with antlers or deer on vases, in glyphs and in ancient texts. Sometimes they were represented with antlers in their hands as an instrument or a staff. This might indicate a relationship with Manik, which means both Hand and Deer. The Wind Seal also has a connection with the Deer. It can be looked upon as the face of a deer with antlers. The Maya described the deer as an animal 'as fast as the wind'.

Activation

During this activating Moon many things will start to kick off. Energy starts flowing. It may give you the feeling of getting something back of the energy you put into projects during the previous Moons. The spark that ignites when energy is activated is what gives this Moon its name: the Electric Moon.

The first day of the Moon = 5 Serpent

Since the first day of the month/Moon gives its energy to the entire month/Moon, one can say that this Moon activates bodily wisdom and passion/Kundalini energy: the qualities of the Serpent. Take your time each day to focus on your body. Do exercises to give your body flexibility, but do it gently. Listen to what your body is trying to tell you, then it will be there to serve you.

Service

This Moons question is: How can I best serve? In the Western world, service has got a negative association. It is easily confused with 'be at service at the expense of yourself'. But that is not what this is about. Service means: creating a heart's connection with the service and compassion of the deer, and taking action. Whenever you empathize with someone, let him/her know. Share it! Ask yourself the following question: How can I best serve the well-being of the world around me: my body, my family, my plants, my work, my purpose?

Dragon Wavespell

Man has a tendency to control, change or improve his environment. This Wavespell is about letting things be the way they are. Do not complain when it rains, but cherish the wet drops falling on your head. Do not get upset in traffic. It is the way it is. Be like a tree that watches the world around it, free of judgement and without wanting to change anything. Cherish life just the way it is. Be your own mother and give yourself what it is you truly need. Cherish your belly and your womb as the source of all life.

Wizard Wavespell

Maybe you already found out in the Dragon Wavespell just how difficult it is to let love really in. This Wavespell is there to sit back and see whatever good presents itself. Feel how difficult it is not to take any action. When something presents itself, dare to let it in. If any questions arise these days, consult your heart where all the answers can be found. Past and future come together in your heart. Try to keep both feet on the ground in order not to be taken over by time-lessness; you might 'lose' a few moments...

Hand Wavespell

'Knowing' is one of the key words of Hand. Hand 'knows' because he is curious and he cannot stand not being in control. Hand wants to 'grab under-standing'. This Wavespell you will be challenged in this area. Maybe there is more than you can or need to understand. Or maybe the right knowledge or teacher will reveal itself/himself. It is now time to literally focus on your hands. Look well after them and let them do what they like to do. Do they want to model clay, do they want to draw, write or massage? Especially creative processes that are manifested through your hands, are healing. Don't give up too easily, this is about accomplishment. To let something be untouched, will not make you happy. It will, however, if you pick it up and deal with it.

day 27
Kin 3

Monday **SEPTEMBER**

18

day 28
Kin 4

Tuesday **SEPTEMBER**

19

Red week of initiation

day 1 *Electric Deer Moon*
Kin 5

Wednesday **SEPTEMBER**

20

SEPTEMBER Thursday

21

day 2
Kin 6

SEPTEMBER Friday

22   Autumn equinox
1103 PM EST

day 3
Kin 7

SEPTEMBER Saterday

23   Autumn equinox
0403 GMT

day 4
Kin 8

SEPTEMBER Sunday

24

day 5
Kin 9

"Always aim at complete harmony of thought and word and deed.
Always aim at purifying your thoughts and everything will be well."
- Gandhi - 10 Human

Red Magnetic Moon Year
Electric Deer Moon

SEP 20 - OCT 17, 2006

notes

day 6
Kin 10

Monday **SEPTEMBER**

25

day 7
Kin 11

Tuesday **SEPTEMBER**

26

White week of refinement

day 8
Kin 12

Wednesday **SEPTEMBER**

27

SEPTEMBER Thursday

28

day 9
Kin 13

SEPTEMBER Friday

29

day 10
Kin 14

○

SEPTEMBER Saterday

30

day 11
Kin 15

○ ○

OCTOBER Sunday

1

day 12
Kin 16

○ ○ ○

---

*"We tend to think that courageous people fear nothing. In reality however,
they are very intimite with fear."*
Pema Chödrön

Red Magnetic Moon Year
Electric Deer Moon

SEP 20 - OCT 17, 2006

notes

---

ooooo **day 13**
Kin 17

Monday **OCTOBER**

2

---

day 14
Kin 18

Tuesday **OCTOBER**

3

Blue week of transformation
Wednesday **OCTOBER**

day 15
Kin 19

4

OCTOBER Thursday

5

day 16
Kin 20
GAP

OCTOBER Friday

6

day 17
Kin 21

OCTOBER Saterday

7

day 18
Kin 22
GAP

OCTOBER Sunday

8

day 19
Kin 23

---

*"The talent for being happy is appreciating and liking what you have,
instead of what you don't have."
- Woody Allen - 9 Mirror*

notes

 day 20
Kin 24

Monday **OCTOBER**

9

day 21
Kin 25

Tuesday **OCTOBER**

10

day 22
Kin 26

Yellow week of ripening
Wednesday **OCTOBER**

11

OCTOBER Thursday

12

day 23

Kin 27

OCTOBER Friday

13

day 24

Kin 28

OCTOBER Saterday

14

day 25

Kin 29

OCTOBER Sunday

15

day 26

Kin 30

---

*"We've got this gift of love, but love is like a precious plant. You can't just accept it
and leave it in the cupboard or just think it's going to get on by itself. You've got to keep
watering it. You've got to really look after it and nurture it.*
- John Lennon - 10 Wizard

Self-Existing Owl Moon 4th Moon of the 13-Moon Year

October 18 - November 14
Totem animal: Owl
Dominant Tone: Tone 4 - measure, define, form

"If you don't know the essence of what is real in this life,
you cannot be creative, you cannot create."
- Pianist Maria João Pires - 1 Warrior

Four is the number with which form is created in the third dimension. Imagine 3 dots in space: a triangle. This triangle exists in one plane. You need at least 4 dots to create a shape, a form. In this third dimension, time is the 4th dimension. Time is necessary to be able to experience the third dimension. Imagine a building. Only by moving through a space, you experience this space, you can estimate its dimensions. You 'measure' by moving your body. Without time - standing still, not using your eyes or ears - you cannot experience the space . It will not become part of your reality. You gain understanding and knowledge by measuring, by orienting yourself in all 4 directions, above and below. Only then will you know where you are. This place forms your reality, the basis from where you move. Anything with 4 as its basis, stands firmly: 4 legs of a table, 4 wheels of a car.
In the 13-Moon Calendar, 4 is the smallest cycle: red, white, blue, yellow. Anything with form can exist by itself. It is something. That's why we call Tone 4 the Self-Existing Tone.

Owl
Man has always feared the night, the darkness and the unknown. The night, however, is the Owl's friend. The Maya used to call the Owl the Night Eagle. Not only can the Owl see in the dark, he can also determine precisely where each

sound comes from and what generated it. That's why the Owl is the totem animal of the 4th Moon, the Moon of the definition of form.

The Owl is our symbol for wisdom, for he can see what others cannot. The Owl sees and understands, where others are blind. You cannot deceive the Owl. When you know where you stand and what your basis is, and when you know what is real and what is not, no one can mislead you.

Many people used to be afraid of the Owl because you couldn't hear him approach. The feathers produce no sound. The owl was often associated with death and the underworld. The Maya knew the mythical Muan bird, who - during the day - accompanied the sun as an eagle, and who - during the night - travelled through the realm of the dead. The Owl has the power of travelling through the unknown. Therefore he is the symbol of many shamans.

Define

Look during this Moon at where you are in your purpose. Ask yourself questions starting with: what, where, when, why and how. What is your basis? What do you have and what do you need and when do you need it? How will you give shape to your actions? Write it down on a piece of paper, or make a model (3 D). Make your thoughts tangible. Only then can it flow.

Hand Wavespell

'Knowing' is one of the key words of Hand. Hand 'knows' because he is curious and he cannot stand not being in control. Hand wants to 'grab under-standing'. This Wavespell you will be challenged in this area. Maybe there is more than you can or need to understand. Or maybe the right knowledge or teacher will reveal itself/himself. It is now time to literally focus on your hands. Look well after them and let them do what they like to do. Do they want to model clay, do they want to draw, write or massage? Especially creative processes that are manifested through your hands, are healing. Don't give up too easily, this is about accomplishment. To let something be untouched, will not make you happy. It will, however, if you pick it up and deal with it.

Sun Wavespell

The Sun represents the universal fire that enlightens and warms all life. Be like the Sun and radiate your love unconditionally into this world. Ask yourself the question how unconditional your deeds really are. What are the hidden motives or expectations? If these are not entirely pure, you might be disappointed this Wavespell. This Solar Seal is also known as a Flower or a Face. Notice how this is presented these days.

Skywalker Wavespell

The Skywalker Wavespell asks you to pay attention. You might be confronted with choices or you might start doubting whether or not you have taken the right path. By being open and perceptive to whatever you come across on your path, you will know whether you have taken the right path or not. The Skywalker is also about courage: the courage to turn around when you realize you took the wrong path, the courage to speak your truth, the courage to leave the safe nest and to discover the world. Keep moving, that is Skywalker's assignment, both in situations and in ideas.

"Those who remain with both feet on the ground, don't get very far", Loesje.

notes

day 27
Kin 31

Monday **OCTOBER**
16

day 28
Kin 32

Tuesday **OCTOBER**
17

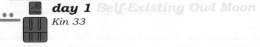

Red week of initiation

day 1 Self-Existing Owl Moon
Kin 33

Wednesday **OCTOBER**
18

OCTOBER Thursday

19

day 2
Kin 34

OCTOBER Friday

20

day 3
Kin 35

OCTOBER Saterday

21

day 4
Kin 36

OCTOBER Sunday

22

day 5
Kin 37

"Don't feel sorry for yourself if you have chosen the wrong road - turn around!"
- Edgar Cayce - 2 Wizard

notes

day 6
Kin 38

Monday **OCTOBER**

23

day 7
Kin 39
GAP

Tuesday **OCTOBER**

24

White week of refinement

day 8
Kin 40

Wednesday **OCTOBER**

25

Red Magnetic Moon Year
Self-Existing Owl Moon

OCTOBER Thursday

26

day 9
Kin 41

OCTOBER Friday

27

day 10
Kin 42

OCTOBER Saterday

28

day 11
Kin 43
GAP

OCTOBER Sunday

29

day 12
Kin 44

"To become different from what we are, we must have some awareness of what we are."
- Eric Hoffer - 13 Star

notes

 day 13
Kin 45

Monday **OCTOBER**

30

day 14
Kin 46

Tuesday **OCTOBER**

31

Blue week of transformation
Wednesday **NOVEMBER**

day 15
Kin 47

1

NOVEMBER Thursday

2

day 16
Kin 48

NOVEMBER Friday

3

day 17
Kin 49

NOVEMBER Saterday

4

day 18
Kin 50
GAP

NOVEMBER Sunday

5

day 19
Kin 51
GAP

"Take at least once a day a time to play."
- anonymous -

notes

day 20
Kin 52

Monday **NOVEMBER**
6

day 21
Kin 53

Tuesday **NOVEMBER**
7

Yellow week of ripening

day 22
Kin 54

Wednesday **NOVEMBER**
8

NOVEMBER Thursday

9

day 23
Kin 55 • • •

NOVEMBER Friday

10

day 24
Kin 56 • • • •

NOVEMBER Saterday

11

day 25
Kin 57 —

NOVEMBER Sunday

12

day 26 ⊠
Kin 58 •
GAP

🌙

*"If you want to know what you think of yourself, then ask yourself
what you think of others and you will find the answer."*
- Seth -

Overtone Peacock Moon

November 15 - December 12
Totem animal: Peacock
Dominant Tone: Tone 5 - command, empower, radiance

Peacock

The Peacock is the totem animal of this Moon, which helps you radiate. He proudly shows his beautiful, shining, blue green appearance, radiating around him like an aura. When will you glow of pride? What do you need to get there?

There's an old Mayan legend about the Quetzal (indigenous peacock). Once upon a time, there was an election among the animals of the jungle. The animal with the most unique features would be crowned king. Kukul, the Quetzal, wanted very much to be king, but he knew he didn't stand a chance, for he was an ugly bird. And so, he came up with a cunning plan: he stole another bird's feathers. He won the election and was crowned king.

In other words, this bird knows very well what it is he needs to maintain his strength, his power. And he also knows how to get it, even though I must advise against theft! The Peacock granted himself power, he em-power-ed himself. He now is one of the most beautiful birds on Earth. What is it you need to maintain your strength, your power?

Overtone Moon

The 4th Moon was still about reality, yet the 5th Moon gets close to magic: the Peacock's tail is so pretty and shiny it almost seems unreal. That's why the Peacock represents the enchantment of the emotional world.

The Peacock also is a symbol of resurrection and immortality. By the time you get to the 5th month, you have resurrected. At Tone 5 you have returned to the direction of the wind where you started off in the cycle of 4: red - white - blue - yellow.

Therefore, Tone 5 is called the Overtone. It inherently creates an intensification of energy when this cycle is added to the previous one. You can use this to strengthen yourself. Empower yourself, show who you really are! However, be aware of your pride. Look at your feet, stay in touch with the ground. As you know, the Peacock has a loud, piercing cry, sharply contrasting his magnificent feathers. According to the Native Americans, it is a cry of dismay. The Peacock is so busy showing his feathers, he forgets how ugly his feet are. Every time he looks at his feet, he cries in dismay...

The first day of the Moon - 9 Dragon
As the first day, the Dragon gives its energy to this month of empowerment. It might do you good to create a safe haven. Cherish yourself within the circle of friends and family. Keep your belly warm and focus on being. This may be precisely what you need to empower yourself.

Skywalker Wavespell
The Skywalker Wavespell asks you to pay attention. You might be confronted with choices or you might start doubting whether or not you have taken the right path. By being open and perceptive to what-ever you come across on your path, you will know whether you have taken the right path or not. Skywalker is also about courage: the courage to turn around when you realize you took the wrong path, the courage to speak your truth, the courage to leave the safe nest and to discover the world. Keep moving, that is Skywalker's assignment, both in situations and in ideas.
"Those who remain with both feet on the ground, don't get very far", Loesje.

quetzal bird

Worldbridger Wavespell
During this Wavespell we continue to let go and forgive: the power of Worldbridger. Before we can enter new paths, we sometimes have to get rid of some lumber. Ask yourself the question whether or not possessions, situations, judgements or ideas still serve you, or whether they keep you from moving on. The Wavespell challenges you, so you can be sure you will encounter everything you need to let go of or forgive. Any resistance is the result of your fear of death. Realize you don't fully live if you can't look at death as a consequence of life.

Storm Wavespell
If - after the previous two Wavespells - there are still things you don't really want to face, the Storm Wavespell will be merciless. It will not be subtle, after all, a soft storm is no storm. Know, however, that this only occurs to purify and trans-form you. If everything remains calm in your life, don't forget you might end up in somebody else's storm. Remain calm. Storm also gives you great power; you have much energy to deal with all sorts of things. Put your shoulder to the tread wheel!

notes

day 27
Kin 59

Monday **NOVEMBER**

13

day 28
Kin 60

Tuesday **NOVEMBER**

14

Red week of initiation

day 1 *Overtone Peacock Moon* Wednesday **NOVEMBER**

Kin 61

15

NOVEMBER Thursday

16

day 2
Kin 62

NOVEMBER Friday

17

day 3
Kin 63

NOVEMBER Saterday

18

day 4
Kin 64
GAP

NOVEMBER Sunday

19

day 5
Kin 65

"I have learnt that the body listens to rhythms that the mind can't even hear."
- John Lee -

notes

day 6
Kin 66

Monday **NOVEMBER**
20

day 7
Kin 67

Tuesday **NOVEMBER**
21

White week of refinement
day 8
Kin 68

Wednesday **NOVEMBER**
22

Red Magnetic Moon Year
Overtone Peaock Moon

NOVEMBER Thursday

23

day 9 🔲
Kin 69 🔲 ° ° ° °
GAP

NOVEMBER Friday

24

day 10 ⊠
Kin 70

NOVEMBER Saterday

25

day 11
Kin 71 °

NOVEMBER Sunday

26

day 12
Kin 72
GAP ° °

"The karmic law requires that every human wish find ultimate fulfillment.
Desire is thus the chain that binds man to the reincarnation wheel."
- Paramhansa Yogananda -

notes

---

day 13
Kin 73

Monday **NOVEMBER**

27

---

day 14
Kin 74

Tuesday **NOVEMBER**

28

---

day 15
Kin 75

Blue week of transformation
Wednesday **NOVEMBER**

29

Red Magnetic Moon Year
Overtone Peaock Moon

NOVEMBER Thursday
30

day 16
Kin 76

DECEMBER Friday
1

day 17
Kin 77
GAP

DECEMBER Saterday
2

day 18
Kin 78

DECEMBER Sunday
3

day 19
Kin 79

"It was like being in the eye of a hurricane. You'd wake up in a concert and think: Wow, how did I get here?"
- John Lennon - 10 Wizard

notes

day 20
Kin 80

Monday **DECEMBER**
4

day 21
Kin 81

Tuesday **DECEMBER**
5

Yellow week of ripening

day 22
Kin 82

Wednesday **DECEMBER**
6

Red Magnetic Moon Year
Overtone Peaock Moon

DECEMBER Thursday

7

day 23
Kin 83

DECEMBER Friday

8

day 24
Kin 84

DECEMBER Saterday

9

day 25
Kin 85
GAP

DECEMBER Sunday

10

day 26
Kin 86

"To live fully is to let go and die with each passing moment, and to be reborn in each new one."
- Jack Kornfield -

Rhythmic Lizard Moon

December 13 - January 9
Totem animal: Lizard
Dominant Tone: Tone 6 - balance, organize, equality

Life is death and death is life. Time is a cycle and a cycle is a rhythm. We experience the movement of the seasons and the passing of time, through the trees losing their leaves. In the middle of the 6th month, the winter solstice is the turning point. On the northern hemisphere we just experienced the darkest period of the year. This is a hard time for many people. Recognition of the cycle of life offers certainty for the return of the light.

Lizard

It's for a good reason that the Lizard is the totem animal of this month. According to a Mexican story, once upon a time the Sun disappeared for 7 days and nights. All the people and all the animals were worried and waited for its return, but in vain. The Sun did not return. A few animals then decided to go and look for the Sun. They searched in rivers, in lakes, in forests and even in the crater of a volcano, but they did not find the Sun. Everybody gave up, except the small green lizard, who kept on searching. She discovers a rock glowing with an inner light. There she found the Sun, sleeping under this rock. She awakens the sleeping sun. The sun returns to the sky, shedding light and warmth on all the earths. Due to Lizards faith and perseverance it was she who brought the Sun back to the world. That's why Lizard is the totem animal for this darkest time of the year.
The Lizard understands the cycle. She is capable of regenerating what was lost. If the Lizard loses his tail, she simply grows another one. This contains a lesson for us. Everything comes and goes... and comes again. This is the Law of Life, the Cycle of Time.

For the Native Americans the Lizard represents the dream. The Lizard knows what is going to happen, for she has already seen it in her dreams. To dream is to go within. This time of year is good for going within and wondering where you stand on your path of life.

Balance

During the 6th Moon you balance what you have set in motion. Outer balance can only exist when there is inner balance. We can find inner balance by traveling to our key, our source. Let's dream, let's equalize outside and inside.

In the Wavespell you change direction at the 5th Tone. The process from 1 to 4 is being repeated from the 5th Tone onward. Just like the stabilization at Tone 2, you rebalance at Tone 5, right after the change of direction. That is rhythm.

Storm Wavespell

The Storm Wavespell will be merciless. It will not be subtle, after all, a soft storm is no storm. Know, however, that this only occurs to purify and transform you. If everything remains calm in your life, don't forget you might end up in somebody else's storm. Remain calm. Maybe by this time of the wavespell the storm has already abated and everything is rebalancing. After the storm it can be unreal calm, like in a dream. Don't be afraid to enter the dream.

Storm also gives you great power; you have much energy to deal with all sorts of things. Put your shoulder to the tread wheel to clean up the mess the storm left behind!

Human Wavespell

Man has Free Will, but do you really want to choose? In the western world, freedom of choice has become a burden. What do I want to eat? What newspaper do I want to read? Whom do I want to see? Where do I want to go? There is so much choice, we often end up in 'who, what, where, which' too soon, skipping the first question: "Do I want to...?" The Solar Seal Human also represents teeth: take well care of your teeth. Pay attention these 13 days to whether or not (and if so, how?) others are trying to influence you. Also pay attention to whether or not you yourself are trying to influence others.

Serpent Wavespell

You may have noticed that the Serpent Wavespell has many GAPs: Galactic Activation Portals. These are intensive days, in which many things can be transformed. It requires a strong focus. The Serpent represents ancient energy, flowing from the Earth up your spine. Your body is the tube, the entrance to the cosmos. Are you comfortable in your body? Does the energy flow without obstructions? Where are your blockades? What is causing them? These days can be filled with extremes: Serpent is both poisonous and base, and it is the symbol of advanced medicine. Listen and dance to the music this Rhythmic Moon. It will help you find the balance!

notes

---

day 27
Kin 87

Monday **DECEMBER**

11

---

day 28
Kin 88
GAP

Tuesday **DECEMBER**

12

Red week of initiation

day 1 *Rhythmic Lizard Moon* Wednesday **DECEMBER**

Kin 89

13

DECEMBER Thursday

14

day 2
Kin 90

DECEMBER Friday

15

day 3
Kin 91

DECEMBER Saterday

16

day 4
Kin 92

DECEMBER Sunday

17

day 5
Kin 93
GAP

---

*"We may explore the universe and find ourselves, or we may explore ourselves
and find the universe. It matters not which of these paths we choose."*
- Diana Robinson -

notes

---

 day 6
Kin 94

Monday **DECEMBER**
18

---

day 7
Kin 95

Tuesday **DECEMBER**
19

White week of refinement

day 8
Kin 96
GAP

Wednesday **DECEMBER**
20

DECEMBER Thursday

21   Winter solstice
      722 PM EST

day 9
Kin 97

DECEMBER Friday

22   Winter solstice
      0022 GMT

day 10
Kin 98

DECEMBER Saterday

23

day 11
Kin 99

DECEMBER Sunday

24

day 12
Kin 100

"I am not an Athenian or a Greek, but a citizen of the world."
- Socrates -

notes

 day 13
Kin 101

Monday **DECEMBER**

Christmas Day **25**

day 14
Kin 102

Tuesday **DECEMBER**

Boxing Day **26**

day 15
Kin 103

Blue week of transformation
Wednesday **DECEMBER**

27

DECEMBER Thursday

28

day 16
Kin 104

DECEMBER Friday

29

day 17
Kin 105

DECEMBER Saterday

30

day 18
Kin 106
GAP

DECEMBER Sunday

31

day 19
Kin 107
GAP

"Let us touch the dying, the poor, the lonely and the unwanted according to the graces we have received and let us not be ashamed or slow to do the humble work."
- Mother Teresa - 1 Sun

notes

 day 20
Kin 108
GAP

Monday **JANUARY**
New Year's Day **1**

 day 21
Kin 109
GAP

Tuesday **JANUARY**
2

Yellow week of ripening

day 22
Kin 110
GAP

Wednesday **JANUARY**
3

JANUARY Thursday

4

day 23
Kin 111
GAP

JANUARY Friday

5

day 24
Kin 112
GAP

JANUARY Saterday

6

day 25
Kin 113
GAP

JANUARY Sunday

7

day 26
Kin 114
GAP

"Time you enjoy wasting, was not wasted."
- John Lennon - 10 Wizard

January 10 - February 6
Totem animal: Monkey
Dominant Tone: Tone 7 - inspire, channel, attunement

Monkey

The Maya made a distinction between the monkeys of the animal kingdom and supernatural God Monkeys, such as Hun Chuen, who granted man the ability to write. The monkeys of the animal kingdom remind the Maya of a period in time they might prefer to forget... The following describes the story of creation from the Pop Wuj, the Sacred Scripture of the Maya.

After Earth had been created with all her plants and animals, the Gods wanted to create beings that would call upon them and worship them. From the soil they created Man. But the soil was soft and it fell apart when it got wet. Creator and Designer then carefully carved sculptures from wood. They seemed like real people and they populated Earth. They got sons and daughters, yet they had no soul and no mind. They walked endlessly on their hands and feet. They were responsible for the animal pets, but treated them badly. They showed no respect towards their environment and destroyed Earth shamelessly. One day, all the animals - large and small - and all the furnishings - pots and pans - revolted against the Wooden Man. And the Gods themselves were discontented. The Wooden Man did not remember its creators, Heart of the Sky and Heart of the Earth. Thus, Heart of the Sky caused a flood, washing away every Wooden Man. The Wooden Man ran for his life. He tried to climb on the roof of his house, but all the houses collapsed. They sought shelter in trees, but the trees shook them off. They fled into caves, but the caves closed themselves. A few Wooden Men managed to flee into the mountains where they still live today as monkeys...

The sacred clown

Even today many people dress up as monkeys during Mayan feasts. Monkeys still have a special function. They make jokes - some of which are quite rude - and tell people what they can and cannot do. They function like the Heyokas of the Native Americans, the sacred clowns. They too teach people about norms and values, by setting a poor example themselves.

Inspiration

This is a Moon to get inspired! The Monkey is a cheerful clown, always ready for a joke. It is the inner child, still without negative experiences, who lets everything flow freely. Let it flow and be inspired! That can lead to wonderful creative processes such as painting and writing. The ancient Maya believed it was the Monkey who gave mankind the ability to write. Ancient images show the Monkey over a book or codex bound in jaguar skin, holding a pen in his hand.

Channel

The Monkey reminds us to attune to the world around us, to be a channel for that. Number 7 is right in the middle between tone 1 and 13. Tone 7 represents the spine, the only joint in the center of your body. It is a channel. And this Moon is very special because we are also in the 7th column of the Galactic Calendar. Be in your center and become a channel. Let energy flow right through you, from top to bottom and back up again. Inspiration will then follow.

Mirror Wavespell

Part of this Wavespell we are in the middle column of the Tzolkin, where future and past join and are reflected in the present. The seal for Mirror is like the Tzolkin. They both looks like a sand-glass. Imagine the pressure at the point where the sand passes the middle. Indeed! It is an intensive period, that will make your heart beat faster and your blood pressure go up. Take extra care if yourself this period.
Mirror reflects. You might be hurt by the shadow side of some people, as they try to pin their problems onto you. Don't be fooled. Search for the truth. In some occasions it will be sufficient to mirror them, to give their problems back to them, where they belong. And naturally, you ask yourself the question whether or not you too pin something onto someone else...

Monkey Wavespell

We are in the middle of the middle; this Wavespell begins right in the center of the calendar. This is where we are closest to Hunab K'u, the source of all life. Many things happen that could make you very serious. Too serious even. If there is a way to please God it will be by happiness and laughter. Day 15 it is Monkey Moon, Monkey Wavespell, Monkey Seal, Monkey Guide. Use Monkey's sense of humor, dare to play and become invincible. Be the light-hearted, spontaneous child. But, stay on the alert, or Monkey will fool you. Be fully grounded in the Here and Now.

Seed Wavespell

Seed is where all talents and abilities meet. What do you need to let that Seed germinate? Create a warm spot in the sun and a good, fertile soil. Manure if necessary. This Wavespell in this Moon, it is time to be inspired and model your sexual and creative life. Be a channel to create. Let the seed sprout! And don't be too impatient, that too is part of the Seed Wavespell.

Red Magnetic Moon Year
Resonant Monkey Moon

JAN 10 - FEB 6, 2007

notes

---

 day 27
Kin 115
GAP

Monday **JANUARY**

8

---

day 28
Kin 116

Tuesday **JANUARY**

9

---

 day 1 *Resonant Monkey Moon*
Kin 117

Red week of initiation
Wednesday **JANUARY**

10

JANUARY Thursday

11

day 2
Kin 118

○

JANUARY Friday

12

day 3
Kin 119

○○

JANUARY Saterday

13

day 4
Kin 120

○○○

JANUARY Sunday

14

day 5
Kin 121

○○○○

"Life is too important to take seriously."
- Corky Siegel -

notes

 day 6
Kin 122

Monday **JANUARY**
15

day 7
Kin 123

Tuesday **JANUARY**
16

White week of refinement

day 8
Kin 124

Wednesday **JANUARY**
17

JANUARY Thursday
18

day 9
Kin 125

JANUARY Friday
19

day 10
Kin 126

JANUARY Saterday
20

day 11
Kin 127

JANUARY Sunday
21

day 12
Kin 128

"Art enables us to find ourselves and lose ourselves at the same time."
- Thomas Merton - 9 Warrior

notes

 day 13
Kin 129

Monday **JANUARY**
22

 day 14
Kin 130

Tuesday **JANUARY**
23

 day 15
Kin 131

Blue week of transformation
Wednesday **JANUARY**
24

JANUARY Thursday

25

day 16

Kin 132 ••

JANUARY Friday

26

day 17

Kin 133 •••

JANUARY Saterday

27

day 18

Kin 134 ••••

JANUARY Sunday

28

day 19

Kin 135 —

"Vision is the art of seeing what is invisible to others."
- Jonathan Swift - 10 Dragon

notes

day 20
Kin 136

Monday **JANUARY**

29

day 21
Kin 137

Tuesday **JANUARY**

30

Yellow week of ripening
day 22
Kin 138

Wednesday **JANUARY**

31

FEBRUARY Thursday
1

day 23
Kin 139

FEBRUARY Friday
2

day 24
Kin 140

FEBRUARY Saterday
3

day 25
Kin 141

FEBRUARY Sunday
4

day 26
Kin 142

"Prayer is exhaling the spirit of man and inhaling the spirit of God."
- Edwin Keith (1958-1990) -

Galactic Hawk Moon

February 7 - March 6
Totem animal: Hawk
Dominant Tone: Tone 8 - model, harmonize, integrity

Galactic Moon

Galactic means: referring to Galaxis, the Milky Way. The Maya looked upon life on Earth as being connected with our solar system and all of the cosmos. Whereas we think the sun rises in the east and sets in the west via the south, the Maya already knew that the Earth itself orbits left counter clockwise and that this is why the sun seems to be moving from left to right. It is as if they looked down on the entire Milky Way from above. That's how their calendar was set up. They knew what we have only recently discovered: the Earth not only orbits around its own axis (24 hours) and around the sun (1 year), but we also orbit - together with the sun - in 26,000 years around the central sun of the Pleiades: Alcyone. To them, our relationship with the Milky Way is part of our every day reality. The 260-day Tzolkin is a fractal of this Great cycle.

Do I live what I believe in?

During the previous Moon you attuned yourself to the Great Spirit and to your surroundings. During this Moon it is time to truly attune your actions to just that, to be in harmony with the Great Spirit, in word and deed. Integrity is when form and contents are in harmony, when you are truly honest. In order to achieve this, you will have to look down onto your life, like a hawk on the wing.

The first day of the Moon = 2 Serpent

The first day of the Moon is a day with solar seal Serpent. This month you will be confronted with the question just how honest you are on an instinctive level.

What do you really need in order to survive? Do you deal with your own body and energy with integrity?

Model
In the cycle of 4 (red, white, blue, yellow), 8 is the intensification of the action of Tone 4. 'To model' is the intensification of 'measuring and defining'. That which you still only observed at Tone 4, is now materialized.

Hawk
The Hawk is the 'Messenger'. The Hawk flies close to the light of Grandfather Sun and brings us the message of the light. The Hawk's shrieking cry enters your subconsciousness and asks you to search for the truth. During the Hawk Moon, you may receive messages from the realm of our Grandfathers and Grandmothers. Open up to these messages and recognize them when you receive them. The power of the Hawk is close to the Skywalker, it is the prophetic messenger. The Hawk flies close to the light of Grandfather Sun. This requires a sharp eye and a bold heart. The Hawk's attentiveness is impressive, he can see from a great distance and looks down on past and future. Be attentive and learn to look at your environment. Observe the ordinary in everything you do. Life gives signs. Life itself is the initiation.

Seed Wavespell
Seed is where all talents and abilities meet. What do you need to let that Seed germinate? Create a warm spot in the sun and a good, fertile soil. Manure if necessary. This Wavespell in this Moon, it is time to be inspired and model your sexual and creative life. Be a channel to create. Let the seed sprout! And don't be too impatient, that too is part of the Seed Wavespell.

Earth Wavespell
This Moons question 'Do I live what I believe in?' might make you stubborn these 13 days. Use the absorbing quality of Mother Earth to let this stubbornness flow into her. Earth will transform your suspicion into faith and she will remind you of your path. You might meet people who are totally convinced of their own ideas and who refuse to let go of them. Are they reflecting what you are doing yourself? Earthquakes may appear out of nowhere, causing major shifts in your work or in your personal life. Don't fight it. Trust it.

Dog Wavespell
Dog is about faith and loyalty, about guiding and being guided. What is it that guides you? Is it good for you? Do you refuse to see something in order to avoid a confrontation? Be in charge of your own life and be loyal to your ideals. What is it you long for? What makes your heart sing? The Mayan word for dog also means feet. Pay attention to your feet, so you don't stub your toe. Feet might very well mean 'to follow' or 'to stand with both feet on the ground'.

day 27
Kin 143

Monday **FEBRUARY**

5

day 28
Kin 144

Tuesday **FEBRUARY**

6

Red week of initiation

day 1 *Galactic Hawk Moon*
Kin 145

Wednesday **FEBRUARY**

7

FEBRUARY Thursday

8

day 2
Kin 146
GAP

• • • •

FEBRUARY Friday

9

day 3
Kin 147
GAP

• • • •

FEBRUARY Saterday

10

day 4
Kin 148
GAP

FEBRUARY Sunday

11

day 5
Kin 149
GAP

"Water is the driving force of all nature."
- Leonardo Da Vinci - 8 Earth

notes

day 6
Kin 150
GAP

Monday **FEBRUARY**

12

day 7
Kin 151
GAP

Tuesday **FEBRUARY**

13

White week of refinement

day 8
Kin 152
GAP

Wednesday **FEBRUARY**

14

FEBRUARY Thursday
15

day 9
Kin 153
GAP

FEBRUARY Friday
16

day 10
Kin 154
GAP

FEBRUARY Saterday
17

day 11
Kin 155
GAP

FEBRUARY Sunday
18

day 12
Kin 156

"There is nothing intelligent about being unhappy."
Arnaud Desjardin

notes

---

day 13
Kin 157

Monday **FEBRUARY**
19

---

day 14
Kin 158

Tuesday **FEBRUARY**
20

Blue week of transformation
day 15
Kin 159

Wednesday **FEBRUARY**
21

FEBRUARY Thursday

22

day 16
Kin 160 • • • •

FEBRUARY Friday

23

day 17
Kin 161 ——

FEBRUARY Saterday

24

day 18
Kin 162 •

FEBRUARY Sunday

25

day 19
Kin 163 • •

"Why does the eye see a thing more clearly in dreams than the imagination when awake?"
- Leonardo da Vinci - 8 Earth

notes

day 20
Kin 164

Monday **FEBRUARY**

26

day 21
Kin 165
GAP

Tuesday **FEBRUARY**

27

Yellow week of ripening

day 22
Kin 166

Wednesday **FEBRUARY**

28

MARCH Thursday
1

day 23
Kin 167

MARCH Friday
2

day 24
Kin 168
GAP

MARCH Saterday
3

day 25
Kin 169

MARCH Sunday
4

day 26
Kin 170

°

"You yourself, as much as anybody in the entire universe, deserve your love and affection."
- Buddha -

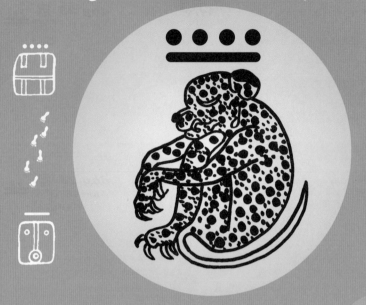

March 7 - April 3
Totem animal: Jaguar
Dominant Tone: Tone 9 - realize, pulse, intention

Jaguar

To the Maya, the Jaguar was a symbol of great strength.
He was associated with the power of the elite. This animal
was so sacred, only high-priests were allowed to wear
robes of jaguar skin. In the spots of the jaguar fur they saw
an image of the starry sky. And we know by now that whoever understands the cycles of the stars, understands the
cycles of the Earth. Even sacrificial altars were made in the
shape of a jaguar, just like the thrones on which the rulers
were portrayed.

The Maya called the jaguar Balaam or Chac (the Rain God).
Balaam also means mysterious or occult. The word Chilam
means a group of priests who explain the oracle and who
predicted the future. The books of the Chilam Balaam are
the Sacred Scriptures of the Mayan priests.

The Jaguar equals Solar Seal Wizard. For
a shaman it is the greatest test and
achievement to transform into a jaguar.
The Jaguar God of the underworld often
appeared as an owl. Maybe that's why
the glyph for Wizard so starkly resembles
an owl.

Solar Moon

During the 9th Moon, the realization of your purpose is getting very close. You can feel the energy pulsating in yourself to bring it into existence here on Earth. However, it is not time yet. After the harmonization with Galaxis we once again return to the Sun in order to get some more energy. That's why this Moon is called the Solar Moon, named after Sol (Sun). You want to charge your intention with solar energy. You are as good as full of that which you are about to realize. The power this emanates is so strong, you would almost forget you still have to manifest your action during the 10th Moon. Before swinging into action, it is wise to once more become the Jaguar who stalks his prey. Consider your options and the details of your plan before you attack. Let the tension of the action pulsate across your fur to the tip of your tail.

The first day of the Moon = 4 Skywalker

When you ask yourself the question: "How do I reach my target?", you can include the energy of the first day of this Moon - the Red Self-existing Skywalker - in your consideration. This is the energy of the Definition of Space.

Dog Wavespell

Dog is about faith and loyalty, about guiding and being guided. What is it that guides you? Is it good for you? Do you refuse to see something in order to avoid a confrontation? Be in charge of your own life and be loyal to your ideals. What is it you long for? What makes your heart sing? The Mayan word for dog also means feet. Pay attention to your feet, so you don't stub your toe. Feet might very well mean 'to follow' or 'to stand with both feet on the ground'.

Night Wavespell

These days you might feel more tired than usual. Go to bed if you want to, it's Dream Time! Write down your dreams. Housing issues might ask your attention these 13 days. If so, give it your attention. This could also be your inner house. Do you feel at home in and with yourself? In the Dream World there is no shortage. Fear of shortage is the opposite of abundance. Don't be tempted to fall back into your fears. The Wavespell challenges you; keep the faith!

Warrior Wavespell

Temptation is near in the shape of beautiful things; you are especially drawn to shining things! It is the Warrior, the Crow and the Vulture in you that make you greedy. Don't be seduced, ask questions instead. Do I really need that? Will that make me happy? Clarify your motivations. You may be a bit confused these days, due to all this questioning. Nothing seems obvious anymore. Be without fear, for it is quite a special state of being when nothing is certain anymore. Enjoy it and don't be too serious.

notes

day 27
Kin 171

Monday **MARCH**

5

day 28
Kin 172

Tuesday **MARCH**

6

day 1 *Solar Jaguar Moon*
Kin 173
GAP

Red week of initiation
Wednesday **MARCH**

7

MARCH Thursday

8

day 2
Kin 174

MARCH Friday

9

day 3
Kin 175

MARCH Saterday

10

day 4
Kin 176
GAP

MARCH Sunday

11

day 5
Kin 177

"Earth laughs in flowers."
- Ralph Waldo Emerson - 9 Human

notes

 day 6 *Kin 178*

Monday **MARCH**

12

 ***day 7*** *Kin 179*

Tuesday **MARCH**

13

White week of refinement
Wednesday **MARCH**

14

day 8 *Kin 180*

MAR 7 - APR 3, 2007

Red Magnetic Moon Year
Solar Jaguar Moon

MARCH Thursday

15

day 9
Kin 181

MARCH Friday

16

day 10
Kin 182

MARCH Saterday

17

day 11
Kin 183

MARCH Sunday

18

day 12
Kin 184
GAP

---

*"I realized that I was planting seeds, and that didn't work. But, if you start giving away
seeds, people will claim their seeds. Some nurture them and grow them,
and that makes a foundational change."*
- Patricia Sun - 4 Monkey

Red Magnetic Moon Year
Solar Jaguar Moon

MAR 7 - APR 3, 2007

notes

---

day 13
Kin 185

Monday **MARCH**
19

---

day 14
Kin 186

Tuesday **MARCH**

Spring equinox
707 PM EST
20

Blue week of transformation
Wednesday **MARCH**

day 15
Kin 187

Spring equinox
0007 GMT
21

Red Magnetic Moon Year
Solar Jaguar Moon

MARCH Thursday

22

day 16
Kin 188

MARCH Friday

23

day 17
Kin 189
GAP

MARCH Saterday

24

day 18
Kin 190

MARCH Sunday

25

day 19
Kin 191

"When I examine myself and my methods of thought, I come to the conclusion that the gift of fantasy has meant more to me than any talent for abstract, positive thinking."
- Albert Einstein - 13 Sun

notes

 day 20
Kin 192
GAP

Monday **MARCH**

26

 day 21
Kin 193

Tuesday **MARCH**

27

day 22
Kin 194

Yellow week of ripening
Wednesday **MARCH**

28

MARCH Thursday

29

day 23
Kin 195

MARCH Friday

30

day 24
Kin 196

MARCH Saterday

31

day 25
Kin 197
GAP

APRIL Sunday

1

day 26
Kin 198

"Life is just a mirror, and what you see out there, you must first see inside of you."
- Wally 'Famous' Amos -

April 4 - May 1
Totem animal: Dog
Dominant Tone: Tone 10 - produce, perfect, manifestation

Manifestation

Finally the time has come. You are ready to realize your purpose and to manifest it here on Earth. It is no longer something that just took shape in your mind, you can now actually touch it. It becomes reality on this planet. That's why we call it Planetary Moon. However, before you get ready, it is wise to include your intention and consideration of the 9th Moon. It might be wise to change it a little here and there. Perfect before you manifest.

Dog

The Dog is the 10th Seal and this is the 10th Moon. The Dog plays an important role in myths and legends in many tribes all over the world. The Maya recognized an enormous dog in the starry sky including the sign of Aries and Taurus. His tail went as far as Cetus (Whale). The Maya called this Dog 'Pek'.
The Key words for the Dog are love and loyalty. This month you are asked to perform your actions from the heart. If you don't do that, your action will miss its purpose and nobody will enjoy it. Is it really what you had in mind when you set your purpose? Does it give you the pleasure and satisfaction you expected? Or does it need some more perfection? Or do you have to let go of the idea that it has to be perfect before you actually manifest? After all, the urge for perfection can hamper your joy of life.
The Dog is an excellent guide, that's why people use guide dogs. Whenever you feel you may have lost your way, call upon the power of the Dog. The Aztecs used to sacrifice a dog and to bury it with the deceased, so it would guide him through

the Underworld. The Dog is also an excellent guard. Even asleep, he will hear every sound and he will guard his territory against intruders. This month you will be asked to take a good look at the borders of your territory. Are there any intruders who need to be growled and barked at? Being loyal to yourself sometimes means being very clear to others. Don't hesitate to show your teeth from time to time.

In the glyph of Dog, the ears are sometimes presented as breasts. The dog then represents all mammals; it is the ability to nurse and to maintain relationship with other kin.

The first day of the Moon = 6 Dragon

The first day of the Moon is Red Rhythmic Dragon: how beautiful for a Planetary Moon of Manifestation! The Red Rhythmic Dragon is the energy of 'equalization' of/to 'birth'. Let your manifestation be like a real birth. Puff, moan and groan and send all your friends a birth announcement card afterwards.

Warrior Wavespell

Temptation is near in the shape of beautiful things; you are especially drawn to shining things! It is the Warrior, the Crow and the Vulture in you that make you greedy. Don't be seduced, ask questions instead. Do I really need that? Will that make me happy? Clarify your motivations. You may be a bit confused these days, due to all this questioning. Nothing seems obvious anymore. Be without fear, for it is quite a special state of being when nothing is certain anymore. Enjoy it and don't be too serious.

Moon Wavespell

Moon deals with feelings and emotions. Moon is universal water: the seas, rivers, the water in your body, the water of the womb, your tears, your sweat. All life needs water. During the Moon Wavespell you may lose it emotionally, with many tears, rage and dramatic behavior. And not just you, so beware! It is wise to purify your body with water. Visit a sauna to sweat, drink a lot of water. Make sure all processes can flow freely through your body. Moon is the power of remembrance. With a well flowing Moon body you will be able to easily feel through people and situations. You know what is true and what is false. You are like an antenna that receives the unspoken words.

Wind Wavespell

These 13 days misunderstandings are just around the corner. You will need to give extra attention to communication. Try to speak clearly and honestly. This Moon year you will hear the unspoken words. Ask questions about it. Is it true? Communicate!

Try to be fully aware of your breathing. What is it you breathe in? In what rhythm? Sacrifice your breath as a gift to the Great Spirit/Hunab K'u, then all your words will flow in this stream. When God created man, he blew life into him with his own breath. Breathe in this Spirit and Inspiration will await you.

notes

day 27
Kin 199

Monday **APRIL**
2

day 28
Kin 200

Tuesday **APRIL**
3

day 1 *Planetary Dog Moon*
Kin 201

Red week of initiation
Wednesday **APRIL**
4

APRIL Thursday

5

day 2
Kin 202

APRIL Friday

6 Good Friday

day 3
Kin 203
GAP

APRIL Saterday

7

day 4
Kin 204

APRIL Sunday

8 Easter Sunday

day 5
Kin 205

"Joy is not in things; it is in us."
- Richard Wagner - 3 Storm

notes

day 6
Kin 206

Monday **APRIL**

Easter Monday **9**

day 7
Kin 207

Tuesday **APRIL**

10

day 8
Kin 208

White week of refinement
Wednesday **APRIL**

11

APRIL Thursday

12

day 9
Kin 209

●

APRIL Friday

13

day 10
Kin 210
GAP

● ●

APRIL Saterday

14

day 11
Kin 211
GAP

● ● ●

APRIL Sunday

15

day 12
Kin 212

● ● ● ●

"Expose yourself to your deepest fear; after that, fear has no power,
and the fear of freedom shrinks and vanishes. You are free."
- Jim Morrison - 8 Moon

Red Magnetic Moon Year

Planetary Dog Moon

APR 4 - MAY 1, 2007

notes

---

 day 13
Kin 213

Monday **APRIL**

16

---

day 14
Kin 214

Tuesday **APRIL**

17

Blue week of transformation

day 15
Kin 215

Wednesday **APRIL**

18

APRIL Thursday

19

day 16

Kin 216

APRIL Friday

20

day 17

Kin 217

APRIL Saterday

21

day 18

Kin 218

GAP

APRIL Sunday

22

day 19

Kin 219

"After a storm comes a calm."
- Matthew Henry -

notes

 day 20
Kin 220

Monday **APRIL**

23

 day 21
Kin 221

Tuesday **APRIL**

24

day 22
Kin 222
GAP

Yellow week of ripening
Wednesday **APRIL**

25

APRIL Thursday

26

day 23
Kin 223 o o

APRIL Friday

27

day 24
Kin 224 o o o

APRIL Saterday

28

day 25
Kin 225 o o o o

APRIL Sunday

29

day 26
Kin 226

"The weak can never forgive. Forgiveness is the attribute of the strong."
- Gandhi - 10 Human

Spectral Serpent Moon

May 2 - May 29
Totem animal: Serpent
Dominant Tone: Tone 11 - release, dissolve, liberation

Serpent

We don't need to wonder why the Serpent is the totem animal of the Spectral Moon of Liberation. The Serpent effortlessly leaves his skin behind so he can continue fully reborn.

The Serpent was the most sacred animal of the Maya, together with the Jaguar. Quetzalcoatl, the Feathered Serpent, was the main God of the Aztecs and the Toltecs. This God is often represented as an upright Serpent (Coatl in the language of the Aztecs), with the beautiful green-blue feathers of the Quetzal bird. He was a deity who - according to legend - truly existed. This divine Serpent descended from Heaven on Earth in order to found a state. He lived a sober life, withdrawn like a priest. He was seduced to a hallucinatory drink and made love with the demonic Goddess of the Mushroom. He subsequently left Earth in a ship made of snake skin, ashamed of what he had done. The rising sun set fire to his ship and his heart flew back to the heavens.

Quetzalcoatl is associated with Venus as the morning star. He is also associated with the Lord of the Winds, who gave life with his breath. This might explain the connection with the Solar Seal Wind, represented as the letter T: symbol of the rattle of a rattlesnake. The rattle can be found high in the sky in the Pleiades.

Release

Personally, I see yet another connection between the Serpent and 'release', in the sense of 'putting into this world'. Once I stayed with friends on a farm. Early in the morning I walked through the garden to a vast pasture, to see the morning haze rise. Still half asleep I stretched out and bowed down to the ground to stretch my legs. With my curls hanging down, I suddenly saw something move. Something was curling, like the curls of my hair. First I just saw one of them, then another one, and yet another one. They were little snakes. My head looked like the head of Medusa! I was startled and got up to check my vision. With my sleepy curly head, I had been hanging upside down in a grass snake's nest, right at the time the babies came out of their eggs. I remembered seeing two large grass snakes earlier that year, living in the dung-hill. It was a magnificent sight: all those baby snakes shooting away from the center, starting a life of their own. What a powerful image: 'releasing', setting free and moving into the world.

That's why this 11th Moon represents letting go and putting into the world whatever it is you manifested during the 10th Moon. Let it live a life of its own, let it follow its own cycle. Feel how free you are from your task. It's done!

Wind Wavespell

These 13 days misunderstandings are just around the corner. You will need to give extra attention to communication. Try to speak clearly and honestly. This Spectral Moon is about Liberation. Is there something you are afraid to say? Speak it out. This Moon year you will hear the unspoken words. Ask questions about it. Is it true? Communicate!

Try to be fully aware of your breathing. Breathe out carefully! Release your breath. Sacrifice it as a gift to the Great Spirit/Hunab K'u, then all your words will flow in this stream. When God created man, he blew life into him with his own breath. Breathe in this Spirit and Inspiration will await you.

Eagle Wavespell

An Eagle Wavespell in a Serpent Moon is typically Mexican. The Mexican red, white and green flag contains an eagle eating a rattlesnake while standing with its left claw upon a nopal cactus. According to an ancient Aztec legend the Aztec people were told by their God Huitzilopochtli that to find their promised land, they were to find the place where an eagle landed on a nopal cactus while eating a snake. After wandering for years, they found the eagle on a swampy island in Lake Texcoco. Here they built what is now called Mexico City.

During the Eagle Wavespell your responsibilities may be pointed out to you. The more you try to escape from them, the more Eagle will fly after you and grab you with his strong claws. His action may seem rough, but didn't you see the web you were caught in? It is for your own good. Eagle asks you to fly with him and to take a look at your own life. See where you are and determine where you want to go. Take a little distance, take a good look and - if necessary - change your direction. And look for signs, like the aztec did, where to land!

Star Wavespell

This is the last Wavespell of the Tzolkin and for a good reason! This is where you can perfect things. Finish your creation, so that it becomes a work of Art. Dissolve your beauty. The shadow of Star is resistance: something your will both encounter and search for these days. You will be focused on your environment and not be in touch much with your inner world. It is wise to radiate inside from time to time, to create enlightenment there as well!

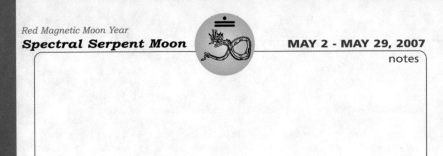

notes

day 27
Kin 227

Monday **APRIL**

30

day 28
Kin 228

Tuesday **MAY**

1

day 1 Spectral Serpent Moon
Kin 229

Red week of initiation
Wednesday **MAY**

2

Red Magnetic Moon Year
Spectral Serpent Moon

MAY Thursday

3

day 2
Kin 230

MAY Friday

4

day 3
Kin 231

MAY Saterday

5

day 4
Kin 232

MAY Sunday

6

day 5
Kin 233

"Your limits are defined by the agreement you once made with yourself about what is possible. Change that agreement and your possibilities will be endless."
- anonymous -

notes

day 6
Kin 234

Monday **MAY**

7

day 7
Kin 235

Tuesday **MAY**

8

day 8
Kin 236

White week of refinement
Wednesday **MAY**

9

MAY Thursday

10

day 9
Kin 237   • • •

MAY Friday

11

day 10
Kin 238   • • • •

MAY Saterday

12

day 11
Kin 239
GAP   •

MAY Sunday

13

day 12
Kin 240   •

"We have all the light we need, we just need to put it in practice."
- Albert Pike - 12 Sun

notes

day 13
Kin 241
GAP

Monday **MAY**

14

day 14
Kin 242

Tuesday **MAY**

15

Blue week of transformation
Wednesday **MAY**

day 15
Kin 243

16

MAY Thursday
17

day 16
Kin 244

MAY Friday
18

day 17
Kin 245

MAY Saterday
19

day 18
Kin 246

MAY Sunday
20

day 19
Kin 247

"The only source of knowledge is experience."
- Albert Einstein - 13 Sun

notes

 day 20
Kin 248

Monday **MAY**
21

 day 21
Kin 249

Tuesday **MAY**
22

Yellow week of ripening

day 22
Kin 250

Wednesday **MAY**
23

MAY Thursday

24

day 23
Kin 251

- - - -

MAY Friday

25

day 24
Kin 252

MAY Saterday

26

day 25
Kin 253

MAY Sunday

27

day 26
Kin 254

· ·

"Life is what happens while you are busy making other plans."
- John Lennon - 10 Wizard

Crystal Rabbit Moon

May 30 - June 26
Totem animal: Rabbit
*Dominant Tone: Tone 12 - **universalize, dedicate, cooperation***

Universalize

After having manifested your purpose during the 10th Moon (or having 'given birth to your child') and after having let go of that purpose during the 11th Moon (or 'let your child breathe on its own'), you now (during the 12th Moon) take a good look at what it is it needs. Give it shelter and a roof above its head. What does it need to take its position in this world? Universalize it. That is this Moon's task. This is what you will dedicate yourself to.

Cooperation

Now you can watch and see how your manifestation relates to the rest. How does it cooperate? This is also a good Moon to get together with other people. It is a time to evaluate. There were 12 knights of the Round Table and Jesus had 12 disciples. Look at the previous Moons. What has been done and how did it go?

Rabbit

Ixchel or Ixquic was the Moon Goddess of the Maya. She is often represented with a rabbit in her arms. Young Ixquic and her son Ixbalanqué often appeared to people as rabbits and hares. In the dark spots on the moon, the Maya recognized the profile of a rabbit. That's why rabbits are Moon animals. They were worshiped by the Maya for their astuteness and their courage. Quite likely, the deed of the Rabbit in the myth of the heroic twins Hunahpú and Ixbalanqué is linked to this courage. When Hunahpú was decapitated by the lords of the Underworld, and his head was exhibited at the place of the ball games, Ixbalanqué made a pumpkin to replace the head of his brother. He asked the Rabbit to sit in a tree, close to the place of the ball games. During the ball game, he shot the ball in the direction of the Rabbit. As agreed, the Rabbit ran away, followed by the lords of the Underworld. Ixbalanqué used this moment to replace his brother's head by the pumpkin. That's how Hunahpú was saved. This is the courageous deed of the Rabbit that is referred to. In our culture, the rabbit is often seen as a fearful being, that freezes when danger appears. He waits before he reacts and runs. But in the story of Alice in Wonderland, it was the rabbit who guided her to the world of magic via holes and tunnels. The Maya called the rabbit 'Tzub'. The star system Rabbit can be found between the rattle of the Serpent and the Turtle. Aldebaran (another star) was his eye.

Crystal-clear
The rabbit has big eyes in the sides of his head. This enables him to have a panorama view of almost 360 degrees, seeing just about everything. He can almost see what's behind him and he can look straight up. The eyes of a rabbit work like a crystal, bundling all the light signals. Be like the Rabbit: let all points of view come together, then everything will become crystal-clear!

Star Wavespell
This is the last Wavespell of the Tzolkin and for a good reason! This is where you can perfect things. Finish your creation, so that it becomes a work of Art. Star's shadow is resistance: something your will both encounter and search for these days. You will be focused on your environment and not be in touch much with your inner world. It is wise to radiate inside from time to time, to create enlightenment there as well! Be Art!

Dragon Wavespell
Man has a tendency to control, change or improve his environment. This Wavespell is about letting things be the way they are. Do not complain when it rains, but cherish the wet drops falling on your head. Do not get upset in traffic. It is the way it is. Be like a tree that watches the world around it, free of judgement and without wanting to change anything. Cherish life just the way it is. Be your own mother and give yourself what it is you truly need. Cherish your belly and your womb as the source of all life.

Wizard Wavespell
Maybe you already found out in the Dragon Wavespell just how difficult it is to let love really in. This Wavespell is there to sit back and see whatever good presents itself. Feel how difficult it is not to take any action. When something presents itself, dare to let it in. If any questions arise these days, consult your heart where all the answers can be found. Past and future come together in your heart. Try to keep both feet on the ground in order not to be taken over by time-lessness; you might 'lose' a few moments...

notes

 day 27
Kin 255

Monday **MAY**

28

---

day 28
Kin 256

Tuesday **MAY**

29

Red week of initiation

day 1 *Crystal Rabbit Moon*
Kin 257

Wednesday **MAY**

30

Red Magnetic Moon Year
Crystal Rabbit Moon

MAY Thursday

30

day 2
Kin 258

JUNE Friday

1

day 3
Kin 259

JUNE Saterday

2

day 4
Kin 260
GAP

JUNE Sunday

3

day 5
Kin 1
GAP

"I am the lizard king. I can do anything."
- Jim Morrison - 8 Moon

notes

 day 6
Kin 2

Monday **JUNE**
4

day 7
Kin 3

Tuesday **JUNE**
5

day 8
Kin 4

White week of refinement
Wednesday **JUNE**
6

JUNE Thursday

7

day 9
Kin 5

JUNE Friday

8

day 10
Kin 6

JUNE Saterday

9

day 11
Kin 7

JUNE Sunday

10

day 12
Kin 8

"I can resist everything exept temptation."
- Oscar Wilde - 9 Worldbridger

notes

···· **day 13**
Kin 9

Monday **JUNE**
11

day 14
Kin 10

Tuesday **JUNE**
12

day 15
Kin 11

Blue week of transformation
Wednesday **JUNE**
13

JUNE Thursday
14

day 16
Kin 12

JUNE Friday
15

day 17
Kin 13

JUNE Saterday
16

day 18
Kin 14

○

JUNE Sunday
17

day 19
Kin 15

○ ○

"Your neighbor's vision is as true for him as your own vision is true for you."
- Miguel de Unamuno - 2 Seed

notes

day 20
Kin 16

○○○

Monday **JUNE**
18

day 21
Kin 17

○○○○

Tuesday **JUNE**
19

day 22
Kin 18

Yellow week of ripening
Wednesday **JUNE**
20

JUNE Thursday

21   Summer solstice
           106 PM EST
           - 1806 GMT

day 23
Kin 19

JUNE Friday

22

day 24
Kin 20
GAP

JUNE Saterday

23

day 25
Kin 21

JUNE Sunday

24

day 26
Kin 22
GAP

"The Breath becomes a stone; the stone, a plant; the plant, an animal; the animal,
a man; the man, a spirit; and the spirit, a god."
- Christian Nestell Bovee - 12 Serpent

Cosmic Turtle Moon

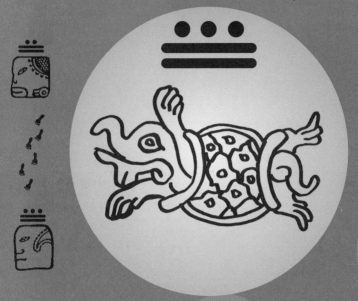

June 27 - July 24
Totem animal: Turtle
Dominant Tone: Tone 13 - transcend, endure, presence

Turtle

This last Moon is a good Moon to think about this year and to rest. Nothing must be done, everything is allowed. The Turtle ('Aak' in the Mayan language) was known for her old age and her patience. That's why she suits this last Moon of the year. Legend has it that the Turtle and the Tree are the wisest grandchildren of Grandmother Galaxy, for they were initiated into the Knowledge of Time for all living beings on Mother Earth. A Turtle carries
the Knowledge of Time on her shell. The inner shell consists of 13 sections, like the 13 Moons of the year. The outer shell consists of 28 sections, the number of days in a month. Yet also in many other cultures, the Turtle is considered a sacred animal, due to her unique qualities: the Turtle is always home, since she carries her house on her back. She is not bound to certain places. She feels at home both in the water and ashore. When there is danger she pulls her head inside her shell, but she also knows that she will have to reach out her neck in order to make her way in this world.
Mayahuel is the Mayan Goddess of Nourishment and Fertility. She is represented in a bearing position, leaning on a turtle. She is the protector

of the womb where all life comes from. That's why she was also called Ayopechtli: 'sitting on a turtle'. The sweat lodge represents both the womb and the Turtle.

Endure
The Native Americans referred to their land as "Turtle Island". Turtle Island is the surface of the earth before it was separated into the continents as we know them today. Legend has it that, when the first conflicts arose between men, Great Mystery decided to purify the Earth with water. The sole survivors after the Great Flood were a man, a few animals and some birds. The man just floated there, all by himself in the great ocean, holding on to a trunk. The Turtle saw the poor man's situation and let him sit on her back. That's how the Turtle became a home for all that lives.

That is precisely what this last Moon of the year asks of you: to be compassionate with every living being and to offer help. Let everything be, in full presence, from a state of inner peace. And with a smile on your face, as the Buddhists say...

Wizard Wavespell
Maybe you already found out in the Dragon Wavespell just how difficult it is to let love really in. This Wavespell is there to sit back and see whatever good presents itself. Feel how difficult it is not to take any action. When something presents itself, dare to let it in. If any questions arise these days, consult your heart where all the answers can be found. Past and future come together in your heart. Try to keep both feet on the ground in order not to be taken over by time-lessness; you might 'lose' a few moments...

Hand Wavespell
'Knowing' is one of the key words of Hand. Hand 'knows' because he is curious and he cannot stand not being in control. Hand wants to 'grab under-standing'. This Wavespell you will be challenged in this area. Maybe there is more than you can or need to understand. Or maybe the right knowledge or teacher will reveal itself/himself. It is now time to literally focus on your hands. Look well after them and let them do what they like to do. Do they want to model clay, do they want to draw, write or massage? Especially creative processes that are manifested through your hands, are healing. Don't give up too easily, this is about accomplishment. To let something be untouched, will not make you happy. It will, however, if you pick it up and deal with it.

Sun Wavespell
The Sun represents the universal fire that enlightens and warms all life. Be like the Sun and radiate your love unconditionally into this world. Ask yourself the question how unconditional your deeds really are. What are the hidden motives or expectations? If these are not entirely pure, you might be disappointed this Wavespell. This solar seal is also known as a Flower or a Face. Notice how this is presented these days.

notes

 day 27
Kin 23

Monday **JUNE**

25

 day 28
Kin 24

Tuesday **JUNE**

26

day 1 *Cosmic Turtle Moon*
Kin 25

Red week of initiation
Wednesday **JUNE**

27

JUNE Thursday

28

day 2
Kin 26

JUNE Friday

29

day 3
Kin 27

JUNE Saterday

30

day 4
Kin 28

JULY Sunday

1

day 5
Kin 29

"If there is magic on this planet, it is contained in water."
- Loren Eiseley - 6 Skywalker

notes

day 6
Kin 30

Monday **JULY**

2

day 7
Kin 31

Tuesday **JULY**

3

White week of refinement

day 8
Kin 32

Wednesday **JULY**

4

JULY Thursday
5

day 9
Kin 33

JULY Friday
6

day 10
Kin 34

JULY Saterday
7

day 11
Kin 35

JULY Sunday
8

day 12
Kin 36

"I am pretty fearless, and you know why? Because I don't handle fear very well;
I'm not a good terrified person."
- Stevie Nicks - 12 Mirror

notes

 day 13
Kin 37

Monday **JULY**

9

 day 14
Kin 38

Tuesday **JULY**

10

Blue week of transformation
Wednesday **JULY**

day 15
Kin 39
GAP

11

JULY Thursday
12

day 16
Kin 40

JULY Friday
13

day 17
Kin 41

JULY Saterday
14

day 18
Kin 42

JULY Sunday
15

day 19
Kin 43
GAP

"If there is something you need, it will come to you, on the condition that you are free.
That is the cosmic law."
- Inti Cesar Melasquez -

notes

 day 20
Kin 44

Monday **JULY**
16

 day 21
Kin 45

Tuesday **JULY**
17

Yellow week of ripening

 day 22
Kin 46

Wednesday **JULY**
18

JULY Thursday
19

day 23
Kin 47

JULY Friday
20

day 24
Kin 48

JULY Saterday
21

day 25
Kin 49

JULY Sunday
22

day 26
Kin 50
GAP

"The beginning of love is to let those we love be perfectly themselves, and not to twist them to fit our own image. Otherwise we love only the reflection of ourselves we find in them."
- Thomas Merton - 7 Mirror

notes

day 27
Kin 51
GAP

Monday **JULY**
23

day 28
Kin 52

Tuesday **JULY**
24

Day out of Time
Kin 53

Wednesday **JULY**
25

Day out of Time

13 Moons of 28 days make 364 days. The one day left is the Day out of Time, celebrated each year on July 25. In the 13-Moon Calendar, July 26 is the first day of the new year. July 25 is the day in between two years, a Day out of Time. It's a day on which connections are made: the old is let go of and the intention for the following year is set. It is a day of being conscious.

The Day out of Time is the 'Galactic Be In', when we celebrate that we are all artists, co-creators of the One Creation as Galactic beings, living as human beings on Earth, together with the four-legged ones, the winged ones, the crawling ones, the finned ones of the waters, the standing ones, the stone people, the plants, the water, air and fire.

This day is a day for peace and culture and is celebrated all over the world. Many thousands of people get together through the power of love and telepathy, in order to let our human culture bloom in harmony with the Earth.

July 25, 2007 - Red Magnetic Skywalker

1 Ben was the seal of Quetzalcoatl, the feathered Serpent. (See Serpent Moon). Quetzalcoatl is a God with a white skin and a dark beard, which was quite unusual for the Maya. According to their prophesy, Quetzalcoatl would return on the day of his Galactic Signature, which was 1 Ben. That is why Cortéz, arriving on a boat (just like Quetzalcoatl) and going ashore on precisely 1 Ben, was considered to be Quetzalcoatl. He was welcomed with a lot of praise and gold. That gold was exactly what the Spaniards were after. We all know how it ended: with the downfall of the Aztec and Mayan empire.

Maybe we may welcome Quetzalcoatl this 1 Ben. They say his coming will be preceded by a comet. Look up while you pray. Who knows...

Visit www.tortuga.com to see whether any feasts are being organized in your vicinity, or be creative and organize your own feast. And you can do the Rainbow Bridge Meditation, download at www.lawoftime.org/law/rainbow.html

Addresses

(Guide)

Name

Address

City

Phone

E-mail

(Guide)

Name

Address

City

Phone

E-mail

(Guide)

Name

Address

City

Phone

E-mail

(Guide)

Name

Address

City

Phone

E-mail

(Guide)

Name

Address

City

Phone

E-mail

(Guide)

Name

Address

City

Phone

E-mail

(Guide)

Name

Address

City

Phone

E-mail

(Guide)

Name

Address

City

Phone

E-mail

Addresses

(Guide)

Name

Address

City

Phone

E-mail

(Guide)

Name

Address

City

Phone

E-mail

(Guide)

Name

Address

City

Phone

E-mail

(Guide)

Name

Address

City

Phone

E-mail

(Guide)

C D

Name

Address

E F

City

Phone

E-mail

(Guide)

Name

Address

City

Phone

E-mail

(Guide)

Name

Address

City

Phone

E-mail

(Guide)

Name

Address

City

Phone

E-mail

Addresses

(Guide)

Name

Address

City

Phone

E-mail

(Guide)

Name

Address

City

Phone

E-mail

(Guide)

Name

Address

City

Phone

E-mail

(Guide)

Name

Address

City

Phone

E-mail

(Guide)

Name

Address

City

Phone

E-mail

(Guide)

Name

Address

City

Phone

E-mail

(Guide)

Name

Address

City

Phone

E-mail

(Guide)

Name

Address

City

Phone

E-mail

Addresses

(Guide)

Name

Address

City

Phone

E-mail

(Guide)

Name

Address

City

Phone

E-mail

(Guide)

Name

Address

City

Phone

E-mail

(Guide)

Name

Address

City

Phone

E-mail

(Guide)

Name

Address

City

Phone

E-mail

(Guide)

Name

Address

City

Phone

E-mail

L M

N O

(Guide)

Name

Address

City

Phone

E-mail

(Guide)

Name

Address

City

Phone

E-mail

Addresses

(Guide)

Name

Address

City

Phone

E-mail

(Guide)

Name

Address

City

Phone

E-mail

(Guide)

Name

Address

City

Phone

E-mail

(Guide)

Name

Address

City

Phone

E-mail

(Guide)

Name

Address

City

Phone

E-mail

(Guide)

Name

Address

City

Phone

E-mail

(Guide)

PQR

Name

Address

S T

City

Phone

E-mail

(Guide)

Name

Address

City

Phone

E-mail

Addresses

(Guide)

Name

Address

City

Phone

E-mail

(Guide)

Name

Address

City

Phone

E-mail

(Guide)

Name

Address

City

Phone

E-mail

(Guide)

Name

Address

City

Phone

E-mail

(Guide)

Name

Address

City

Phone

E-mail

(Guide)

Name

Address

City

Phone

E-mail

(Guide)

Name

Address

City

Phone

E-mail

UVW

(Guide)

Name

Address

XYZ

City

Phone

E-mail

Credits & books

Text:
We thank José Argüelles, Tortuga, Aluna Joy Yaxk'in, Eden Sky, Peter Toonen, Mike Floris, Jamie Sams and Rita van Vliet.

Illustrations:
Nicole E. Zonderhuis
Blue Moon by Kostian Iftica from - http://science.nasa.gov
(Kostian Iftica - www.explorethecosmos.com)
Background cover - NASA, ESA and S. Beckwith (STCcI) and the HUDF Team
Tortuga - for the Solar Seals, Hunab K'u, the Hunab K'u with seals and tones, the Foundation logo and the Day out of Time Rainbowbridge.
Famsi - drawings of Linda Schele and photos of Justin Kerr.

Images are found in different books and websites, but they are originally Mayan (credits to the Maya!). We found out that many images are first published by FAMSI, Foundation for the Advancement of Mesoamerican Studie, Inc. where you can find a database of the drawings of Linda Schele and photos of Justin Kerr.

We have done every effort to trace down and represent all possible sources. In case we did not succeed, we are sorry and please let us know: info@mayatzolkin.com

BOOKS

Mayan Astrology - A User Friendly Guide to Mayan Astrology
> by Aluna Joy Yaxkin
Medicine Cards - the discovery of power through the ways of animals
> by Jamie Sams and David Carson
El Zodiaco Maya by Hugh Harleston
The story of Time; the story of Turtle and Tree by José Argüelles
The Mayan Oracle - Return Path to the Stars
> by Ariel Spilsbury & Michael Bryner
Dreamspell: - The Journey of Timeship Earth 2013
> by José Argüelles
Telektonon: The Prophecy of Pacal Votan
> by José Argüelles
Earth Ascending - An Illustrated Treatise on the Law Governing Whole Systems
> by José Argüelles
The Mayan Factor - Path Beyond Technology
> by José Argüelles
Surfers of the Zuvuya: Tales of Interdimensional Travel
> by José Argüelles
The Arcturus Probe -Tales and Reports of an Ongoing Investigation
> by José Argüelles

Most of the above books are also available at:
Frontier Sciences Foundation: www.fsf.nl
Adventures Unlimited Press: www.adventuresunlimitedpress.com

For more books by José Argüelles, see
www.lawoftime.org/content/bookstore-books.html
www.thirteenmoon.org/body%20text/catalog.htm

*Go to www.mayatzolkin.com for a list of clickable links and updates.
If you have an interesting website about the 13-Moon Calendar or Maya,
please send us an e-mail: info@mayatzolkin.com*

Official sites:
*13-Moon Calendar Change Peace Movement: www.tortuga.com
The Invisible College: www.earthascending.com/maya/index.html
Foundation For The Law of Time: www.lawoftime.org*

13-Moon / Tzolkin websites:
*José Argüelles - www.earthascending.com
Ariel Spilsbury - cosmicircus.com
Eden Sky - www.13moon.com
Aluna Joy Yaxk'in - www.kachina.net/~alunajoy
Starroot - www.starroot.com/cgi/daycalc.pl + www3.telus.net/starroots
Randy Bruner - http://home.earthlink.net/~cosmichand/index.html
MonkeyScribe - www.galactichardwarestore.com
John Major Jenkins - http://edj.net/mc2012/fap6.html
Jay - www.geocities.com/SoHo/7331/dreamspell.html
Willard Van De Bogart - www.earthportals.com/Portal_Messenger/arguelles.html
Atmara Rebecca Cloe - www.nwcreations.com/13mooncalendar.htm
Crossroads - www.lucidcrossroads.co.uk/mayan.htm
Tracey Gendron - www.astrodreamadvisor.com*

Other:
*www.pauahtun.org/Calendar/Default.htm - complex insights into the calendars
www.halfmoon.org
www.synchronometer.com
www.2012.com.au
www.13mooncalendar.com*

Planet Art Network:
*PAN Holland - www.panur.nl, www.pan-holland.nl, www.mayatzolkin.com
PAN Scotland - www.spirit-of-yggdrasil.com
PAN United Kingdom - www.wavespell.net
PAN Oregon - www.thirteenmoon.org
PAN Australia - www.timeisart.net
PAN Brasil - calendariodapaz.com.br
PAN Colombia - www.pancolombia.com
PAN Spain - www.13lunas.net
PAN France - tortuga.usebynet.com
PAN Hungary - rinri.hu/tiki-index.php
PAN Italia - digilander.libero.it/panitalia
PAN Japan - www.panlibrary.org
PAN Jugoslavija - iklamat.on.neobee.net
PAN Russia - iklamat.on.neobee.net
PAN Uruguay - uruguay.tortuga.com*

See www.tortuga.com/pan/nodes.html for more PAN links

Notes

Stick-a-pocket

glue glue glue glue glue glue glue glue glue glue glue glue glue glue glue glue glue glue glue glue

Cut, glue *and* stick.

glue glue glue glue glue glue glue glue glue glue glue glue glue glue *stick stick stick stick stick stick stick stick stick stick stick stick stick stick stick stick stick stick stick stick*

stick stick stick stick stick stick stick stick stick stick stick stick stick

Notes

Who we are

Sylvia Carrilho

"Since my contact with the Mayan calendars, I accelerated in a synchronized flow. As a working mother, raised with Gregorian customs, I have always had the urge to make manageable 'tools' for natural time in day-to-day life.
To support my integration/transformation, I developed the Tzolkin Day Seals as a sticker and the 13-Moon (menstrual) cycle calendar, which you can also download as a PDF from the mayatzolkin website. Synchronicity is leading my development of more natural time tools like the 13-Moon Diary.
I'm open for questions, remarks, advice, ideas and stories to support our change in time."

In Lak'ech
Sylvia Carrilho

Nicole E. Zonderhuis

Since her travels through Mexico and Guatemala, Nicole studied and lives according to the 13-Moon Calendar. She is a designer/artist and writer, holding workshops about the 13-Moon Calendar in Holland and Europe, with a focus on the experience and practice in daily life. Day by Day in the Mayan Way!

"I studied Art, Landscape and Architectural Design. I was so fortunate to have a teacher who made me aware that it is possible to read a location before designing; many times the place asks us for a certain type of use. Studying the architectural history, you find that monuments are placed on locations with a strong energy and many times a legend arose concerning the site. I visited power places in Europe; standing stones and stone circles in France and England like Stonehenge, churches built on old sacred sites, places with stories like the Arthur legend in Tintagel. I felt that sometimes a place was so happy to get focused attention that I felt the urge to bring people together on these sites. First, I used architecture and art as the medium. But later I sensed that people are looking for a way to express themselves on power places. We have forgotten the ceremonies; we have forgotten how to pray and how to act. It was painful to see the uneasy behavior of the people at the sacred fountain in the forest in Brittany. But who am I to stand up and guide them?
Well, I am 10 BEN, Red Planetary Skywalker. The affirmation for Skywalker is: "I am your messenger of the Light. I give to you the ability to travel through time and space." As a Skywalker I am the messenger, and sometimes the ropedancer, balancing high in the sky. Tone 10 is about Manifestation. People with Tone 10 change raw material and information into something visible and tangible. For me, to be 10 Ben, is about giving shape to the unseen connections, to the message. In WebCraft, my work as a designer/artist, but also with the MoonCraft activities, like the moon-ceremonies and 13-Moon Calendar workshops, I bring people closer to their inspiration and make the cosmic connection tangible."

In Lak'ech
Nicole E. Zonderhuis

About her activities, see www.mooncraft.nl and her design, see www.webcraft.nl

The Stone Puzzle of Rosslyn Chapel

Philip Coppens

Learn the Truth behind its Templar and Masonic Secrets... and why this small chapel was featured in *The Da Vinci Code*.

The Canopus Revelation

Philip Coppens

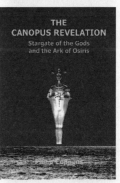

The Southern Polar star was a stargate of the Gods, but also the Ark of Osiris, from where he was resurrected.

Nostradamus and the Lost Templar Legacy

Rudy Cambier

Just outside of Brussels, the Templars may have hidden part of their treasure... and Nostradamus may have known it.

The Templars' Legacy in Montreal, the New Jerusalem

Francine Bernier

The Canadian town was built by Lazarist priests, incorporating knowledge that was suppressed in France

from Frontier Publishing

Saunière's Model and the Secret of Rennes-le-Château

André Douzet

Discover the secret the enigmatic priest tried to encode at the end of his life... only to fail, until in the early 1990s, his final message was retrieved.

The Wanderings of the Grail

André Douzet

The French Pyrenees have long been connected with myths of the Grail... But the Cathar tradition has continued into the 20th century....

The Secret Vault

Philip Coppens & André Douzet

Notre Dame de Marceille harbours an enigmatic network of underground tunnels, which intrigued the main players of the mystery of Rennes-le-Château... why?

Egypt: Image of Heaven

Willem H. Zitman

The astonishing revelation as to how and why the ancient pyramid field was built in ancient Egypt... and how it traces its design back to an even earlier civilisations, with traces in the Sahara.

from Frontier Publishing